I AM Smart

A Guide To Recognizing And Developing Your Child's Natural Strengths

By
Dawna Markova, Ph.D. & Angie McArthur

This book is intended as a reference volume only, not as a medical manual. The information given here is designed to help you make informed decisions about your child's intellectual development and behavior. It is not intended as a treatment or substitute for medical treatment. The names and identifying characteristics of all children and parents mentioned have been changed.

Copyright © 2015 by Dawna Markova, Ph.D. and Angie McArthur

All rights reserved.

Published in the United States by SmartWired LLC, Park City, UT.

ISBN 978-0-9725655-1-6

1. Child psychology. 2. Self-actualization (Psychology) in children 3. Success in children. 4. Learning ability. 5. Child rearing. 6. Parenting. I. Title.

Printed in the United States of America

www.smart-wired.com

Graphic conceptualization: Angie McArthur
Graphic design: John Vieceli
Editor: Heather McArthur

First Edition
9 8 7 6 5 4 3 2 1

FOREWORD

By the co-authors of The Spiritual Dimension of Leadership, Dr. Paul D. Houston, executive director of the American Association of School Administrators, and Dr. Stephen L. Sokolow, executive director of the Center for Empowered Leadership

We (Paul and Steve) both are parents and grandparents as well as lifelong teachers and leaders in public education. In all of those roles we wanted the same thing for the children we served as we did for our own children and grandchildren—the gift of empowerment. We also wanted to learn who we were and where we fit in the world. We wanted to learn what we had to offer and how to best use the innate gifts and talents we had been given. That's what all people want. But how do we go about it? That's what this remarkable book you now hold in your hands is about—discovering our innate gifts, and then cultivating and sharing them. At a deeper level this book is about making the world better by bringing out the best in each and every parent's child—bringing out the best in your child.

Gifts come in all shapes and sizes. Some are innate, waiting for us to discover them and give them a means of expression. Others are already on the outside for us to see and feel. When you first think about gifts, it is usually about something that you have received that was meaningful to you. Then you might think about something you have given to someone else. But the true power of giving resides in the intention of the giver, and this is the gift you get to share with yourself.

There was a teacher who was working on an isolated island in the South Pacific. There were few things of worth on the island, but it was known for a special kind of shell that could be found on a remote beach. The teacher commented to her class that someday she hoped to walk to that beach so she could have one of the shells. A few days later, one of the students came in and placed one of the shells on the teacher's desk. The teacher was touched but told the student, "You shouldn't have walked that long distance just to give me this shell." The child replied, "But, teacher, the walk was part of the gift."

As educators we have always loved that story, for it is the task of teachers and parents to make that long walk on behalf of our children. But what constitutes the right path?

When we first met Dawna Markova, it was quickly apparent that she was a gift to us from the universe. Dawna is an incredibly talented woman whose engaging life force exudes a powerful radiance. She is a natural storyteller, and we wanted to hear her story. We wanted to know everything about her. Instead, she focused on us, on what we were doing, shedding light on our story. As she did so, we were uplifted and empowered. It was as if she were holding up a magic mirror, reflecting back to us the best that was in us. She also showered us with gifts of books, poems, and prayers—even a crystal bowl. But the real gift was the gift of her presence, of her being. Being around Dawna leads you to understand that with her, the gift is in the walk. She makes life special by giving her shells to others.

Dawna has brought her poetry and passion to the world. She has inspired hundreds of thousands to give to others through the Random Acts of Kindness movement that she helped spawn. And now she is embarking on her greatest walk—to help the world understand the innate gifts that our children bring to us.

We all have a mother, the person who brought us into this world, the person from whom we first learned love and trust, and in whose eyes we first learned to see ourselves. Dawna Markova is the embodiment of the Universal Mother, the universal nurturer who helps us to become our best self. She has an abundance of love and wisdom and a burning passion to help each of us reach our fullest potential. She empowers us and helps us to identify and nurture our unique spark, our unique gifts and talents.

This extraordinary woman of wisdom is our teacher and guide, a role model who can show us how to be the parents we want to be and how to create for our children what we most want for them—the opportunity to be who they really are and add their special strand to the evolving fabric of life.

This book is a living prayer, a blessing to every parent and every child, and to life itself.

TABLE OF CONTENTS

Introduction ... 7

PART 1:
GETTING SMART ABOUT BEING S.M.A.R.T. ... 11

   Chapter One:
   Parenting: *A Journey that Begins with You* ... 12

   Chapter Two:
   The Four Guiding Principles ... 21

   Chapter Three:
   S.M.A.R.T: The Power of Thinking Differences ... 28

PART 2:
THE SMART PARENTING PROCESS: *HOW TO RECOGNIZE AND DEVELOP THINKING DIFFERENCES* ... 31

   Chapter Four:
   Successes: *Identify and Track What Works* ... 32

   Chapter Five:
   Mind Patterns: *Identify How Your Child Best Uses Attention to Focus, Sort, and Imagine* ... 37

   Chapter Six:
   Attractions and Interests: *Identify and Motivate with What Your Child Naturally Loves to Do* ... 53

   Chapter Seven:
   Resources: *Identify and Succeed with People, Places, and Things that Bring Out Your Child's Best* ... 57

   Chapter Eight:
   Thinking Talents: *Identify and Develop the Ways Your Child Thinks that Makes Him or Her Unique* ... 62

PART 3:
THINKING PARTNERSHIPS THROUGHOUT THE JOURNEY ... 77

   Chapter Nine:
   Drawing Support from Teachers, Coaches, Mentors, and Yourself ... 78

   Chapter Ten:
   Taking It Further: Additional Tools and Tips ... 82

How did this work begin? Remembering my muse

— Dawna Markova, Ph.D.

> *"Imagine a world in which every child understands what his or her natural strengths and talents are, how he or she learns and communicates most effectively, and how he or she thinks most effectively with others. If you can imagine it, then you can help create a world worthy of your children."*
>
> —Dawna Markova, Ph.D.

Jerome, a young man I was privileged to meet in a Florida school several decades ago, was labeled as "retarded" and "resistant" instead of…well, let me tell you a story about Jerome.

He was a six-foot-tall, black, 14-year-old sixth grader living in a migrant labor camp with his mother and two sisters. I was the "learning specialist." My office was the former broom closet. The principal referred Jerome to me on the day school opened. "Just keep him out of trouble. He'll never be able to learn to read; he's trainable, not educable. Train him to behave in my school."

Jerome's cumulative folder was full of labels listing all of his deficits and disorders. His deep eyes held both mischief and misery. He told me the first day not to bother trying to teach him, because he wasn't ever going to read. That made it almost unanimous—and a challenge.

I learned from Jerome's mother that he was the chess champion of the migrant camp. I went to watch him play one night, which was evidently rather unusual. No teacher had ever done such a thing. I found Jerome surrounded by a small crowd, sitting on boxes or squatting. As Jerome paced, no one made a sound. His eyes scanned the board, and then, suddenly, he pounced. "Checkmate!"

I had an idea. I brought a large book to my office; its title, *A Black History of America*, was spelled out in gold letters. Jerome, who had never seen a book with photographs of African Americans, did everything he could to try to get me to read it to him. Finally, I offered to play a game of chess with him, but only on these conditions: If he won, I'd read the book to him. If I won, he'd have to learn to read it.

It must have been divine intervention: I was a mediocre chess player and Jerome was an expert, but I won that game. It took us the rest of the school year, but Jerome did learn to read that book. We explored the pattern his mind used when he played chess, and figured out how to use that pattern to help him read.

"I need to be standing and moving. It's gotta be real quiet so I can think. Then I have to look steady with my eyes at the whole board until I can see it in my mind. After that, a voice way inside tells me what to do."

While he moved, I traced words on his back. He'd say them while he looked at the book, then write them on paper. It was laborious, but Jerome learned very quickly. He taught me as much as I taught him.

On his last day of school, he disappeared, leaving the book behind, even though I had given it to him as a celebration present. His mother told me he was afraid it would get stolen, and that would hurt too much. She handed me a poem he had written for me:

I don't know
how to show
the delight of feeling right
about what was wrong
or so they said
with my head.
Thanks.

I feel despair when I hear someone say how children are "unmotivated" and "resist learning." They may be resistant to being taught, but not to learning.

Every parent I have every worked with, has asked a simple questions without a simple answer, "Is there an instruction manual that would teach me what I can do to makes sure my child will be ready to face any challenge?"

What if I told you it's not an instruction manual that's needed, but a guide you partner with your child to create? An intellectual "Tracker" that could grow as he or she does. Each year, as your child learns and tries new things—you could track what they love. What ignites and inspires.

Think about what's tracked in today schools? A record is kept and passed on from teacher to teacher, year after year, about what the child struggles with, what is hard for him or her. Imagine if your new car or computer came only with instructions on what its limitations were and what not to do! Chances are you'd never leave your driveway.

When I was a classroom teacher, I was equally frustrated with all the information about what didn't work with the children in my classroom that I decided to take the matter into my own hands. I hung large sheets of newsprint, one for each child, on the walls of my classroom. I invited anyone who knew anything about what did work with that child, be they coaches, other teachers, siblings, grandparents, friends, to add it to his or her "Smart Passport." After seven days, I typed up all the newsprint and handed each parent an instructional manual, asking that they, as the ultimate champion, make sure it was updated each year and shared with all teachers.

It is fifty years later. Amazingly enough, on occasion I get an email from one of those students, now grown with children of their own. What gives me the most satisfaction is hearing that, because of those Smart Passports, their knowledge of how they are smart has continued to help them face challenges and realize their potential.

It is now time to empower parents around the world to understand how to do what I did five decades ago. My colleague and co-author Angie McArthur, who is also my daughter-in-love, now brings this legacy to you with me in the form of this book. It will enable you to create a Smart Passport for each of your children.

This book will help you to create a Smart Passport for each of your children. It is like a hand on your back, guiding you as you guide them to apply their unique ways of learning and talents to whatever challenge they face. We have learned a great deal since that classroom with the newsprint-covered walls. As you will discover in the pages that follow, we've created more specific and informative ways of increasing awareness of strengths and talents that make the Smart Passport even more helpful. The underlying intention though is still the same: to help each child recognize and share the unique talents that only he or she can bring to the world.

Part 1:

GETTING SMART ABOUT BEING S.M.A.R.T.

"When you know better, you do better."
—Maya Angelou

CHAPTER ONE

Parenting: A journey that begins with you

"We never know the love of the parent till we become parents ourselves."

—Henry Ward Beecher

Think about every baby who is born. They come into this world vulnerable little vessels ready to be filled. When you hold an infant in your arms, you feel it—that wonder and amazement as you look at the prints at the ends of those tiny fingers. You become aware of how this child is the result of so many people's dreams and prayers. You realize that it could be possible for this child to do something remarkable, something that makes a difference to the rest of us. Perhaps, in that moment and a thousand times since, you've asked yourself how you could best support this precious child so that he or she could thrive.

The possibilities are endless: each baby will become a child and then an adult with the ability to create, discover, imagine, communicate, and analyze. Each child has the capacity for virtue, compassion, love, goodness, and reason. Yet, in the busyness of daily life and all the challenges of parenting, we tend to forget about their unique brilliance. Too often the door closes and the focus of our attention shifts—from natural gifts that need to be developed, to what is wrong that needs to be fixed. When we do this, we limit what could be possible for our children. We see Kevin as "hyperactive" instead of energetic. We call Leanne "inattentive" instead of imaginative. We label Javier "oppositional" rather than independent. Jennifer is described as being "oversensitive," not empathetic.

As the parent or caregiver you play a critical role
Your child's brain, emotional resilience, responses, and physical development are not "pre-programmed" in the womb but impacted by the environment they are born into and the care given. The number one determinant to how your children "turn out" as an adult is how they are nurtured and supported in the early years. Research has proven that a key factor in a child's intellectual and emotional development is responsive and supporting relationships with parents and other caregivers. According to the web site childwelfare.gov, an infant's brain develops best when a few stable caregivers work to understand and meet the infant's need for love, affection, and stimulation. Additionally, if babies continue to receive consistent affection and support from these caregivers, they'll develop into children, teens, and adults who are happier, healthier, and possess critical relational and problem-solving skills. In his book, *The Whole Brain Child*, Dr. Daniel Siegel explains how a child's developing brain actually "mirrors" his or her parent's brain. As parents become more aware and emotionally healthy, their children reap the rewards and move toward health as well. As Siegel points out, "Integrating and cultivating your own brain is one of the most loving generous gifts you can give your children."

> *"As you hold your infant in your arms, you feel as if a door inside your hearts opens—you feel a wave of wonder at the miracle of this child's potential."*
>
> —Dawna Markova, Ph.D.

Napoleon Hill, author of Laws of Success, says we become like the people we associate with. If children associate with loving, kind, giving people they tend to grow up having similar traits. In fact, children are greatly influenced by how caregivers navigate, react to and deal with the day-to-day details of their lives. Young children tend to come into newly formed families, with parents who are just learning how to communicate in relationship with each other. If happiness is the relaxed enjoyment of life, it takes a lot of reframing to find be able to relax amidst crying children, sleepless nights, or a partner that seems unsympathetic.

> *Martin Seligman, one of the founders of "positive psychology" (according to which, in order to gain enjoyment from existence, one cannot merely neutralize negative and afflictive emotions – one must also promote the birth of positive emotions), asked thousands of parents the following question: "What is the thing you want most for your children?" For the best part, their responses were: happiness, self-confidence, joy, pleasure, thriving, equilibrium, kindness, health, satisfaction, love, balanced behavior, and a life full of meaning. In summary, well-being is the first thing that comes to parents' minds for their children.*
>
> *Seligman's next question to the same parents is "What do we teach at school?" to which the response came: the ability to think, the ability to fit into a mold, language and math skills, work ethic, the capacity to pass examinations, discipline and success. The answers to these two questions barely overlap at all. The qualities taught at school are undeniably useful and for the most part necessary, but school could also teach ways of achieving well-being and self-fulfillment; in short, what Seligman calls a "positive education," an education which also teaches every student how to become a better human being.*
>
> — Matthieu Ricard, philosopher, scholar,
>   Buddhist monk known as "The happiest person in the world."

With our children we must be the parent we want them to grow up to be. If we want them to be full of virtue and love we must reflect virtue and love. Research from studies on early childhood intervention tells us that ninety percent of the brain is developed by the time our child is age five. How she handles challenges, relates to boys as a teen, looks at drugs, food, and consuming alcohol as an adult will be most affected by how she is nurtured, supported, cared for and connected to her caregivers. In fact, ample research proves that nurturing children—starting from the first trimester—sets the foundation for them to enter kindergarten ready to learn and thrive. The sixty-year "Head Start" study focuses on six key factors needed to support a child's development well before they enter the classroom. Although instinctively we do many of these, this checklist is a good reminder to make sure each one stays forefront in our awareness as we navigate the early years.

Six foundational factors for early childhood development

1 An intention to create and maintain a culture and environment where your child feels connected, valued, respected, and loved, and where your child's talents and abilities are nurtured so he or she can thrive physically, emotionally, spiritually, and mentally.

2 **Physical safety:** Your child's environment is safe. Your child gets plenty of rest, is fed healthy food, is exposed to little or no "screen time" (i.e. TV, tablet, etc.), has regular visits to the doctor and is immunized.

3 **Emotional safety:** Your child's environment feels safe, warm, comforting, and is free from people, music, videos, games, or movies exhibiting anger, depression, drug and alcohol abuse, or violent behaviors.

4 There is an ongoing connection to caring cooperative, loving, disciplined adults, whose intention is to create and maintain a culture and environment where your child feels connected, valued, respected, and loved.

5 As a parent or caregiver you have support from your church, community, employer, family and/or friends, helping you concentrate on giving time to your child. There is no substitute for time and you need others to help support you in giving time and attention to your child.

6 Parenting and caregiver education. You should have access and support to books, videos, classes, mentors and other resources regarding your child's development, healthy living, and your parenting.

It's not how smart your child is, it's how he or she *is* smart

From when you first hear the news you're going to be a parent to the day they start life and beyond, you're focused on providing an environment where your child is loved and supported. As a parent, grandparent, or caregiver, the hope remains the same: we all want our children to succeed. We want them to be who they are meant to be in this world and to know that they make a difference. We desperately want them to navigate smoothly through school, to make good choices, to have great friends, and eventually live a healthy, happy, balanced life. So, how can you equip them with what they need to achieve this?

I Am Smart is here to help. This book will guide you through identifying your child's own success formula—a blueprint that empowers them to know how they are uniquely smart. With this knowledge, your child has what he or she needs to overcome challenges and create success in school and in life.

This is what we call an asset-focused approach to learning. It is where you focus on helping your child use his or her natural strengths to overcome limitations. This approach weaves together foundational concepts developed by our fifty-plus years of cognitive research, refined and tested with families, schools, and learning organizations around the world.

I Am Smart facilitates a learning partnership between you as a parent (or caregiver) and your child so he or she discovers the unique way to think and learn most effectively. While there are countless parenting books that focus on skills and techniques, very few center on what's needed to equip our children to truly succeed. Designed to be used for kids starting at age five right through to eighteen, the universal concepts in *I Am Smart* can be applied to any age by imagining the possibilities the following two questions evoke:

1. **What if every child in the world is seen as a valued resource to be developed rather than a problem to be solved?**

2). **How can we give our children, and ourselves, the best by unleashing the potential that exists within each of us?**

With these two questions at the forefront, *I Am Smart* is designed to guide you through a process of discovery. Together with your child, you'll create a database of powerful information centered on what he or she loves and is naturally good at. As a result, you'll have your own Smart Passport—an evolving profile designed to help you and your child document the most effective ways for them to learn and excel. This tool highlights their very own unique gifts, talents, and abilities and other critical information that can be shared with caregivers, teachers, coaches, tutors, and mentors—so everyone understands the best way to help your child succeed.

This book will help you to create a Smart Passport for each of your children. It will guide you as you guide them to apply their unique ways of learning and talents to whatever challenge they face. We have learned a great deal since that classroom with the newsprint-covered walls. As you will discover in the pages that follow, we've created more specific and informative ways of increasing awareness of strengths and talents that make the Smart Passport even more helpful. The underlying intention is still the same: to help each child recognize and share the unique talents that only he or she can bring to the world.

Creating a rich learning environment

Why is tracking all this information necessary? The answer can be found in a simple formula developed by best-selling author and coach, Timothy Gallwey. It can be applied in school, sports, or at work: p = P – i, where the lower case "p" means performance, the capital "P" means potential, and the "i" means interference.

performance equals POTENTIAL minus interference

Interference can be external—including anything that leads to your child feeling shamed, threatened, or deprived of positive feedback. Other external interferences include loud noises, time constraints, or similar distractions. Interference can also be internal, such as self-blame or thoughts like "I am stupid," or "I can't do this."

When your child is able to identify and raise awareness to the kinds of interferences that impact his or her learning, as a parent you can help minimize them. With these and other actionable insights illuminated in the Smart Passport, you'll have what's needed to help your child reach his or her potential.

Unlocking potential in every child also comes from understanding the need for a diverse learning environment, one that includes novelty, challenge, feedback, physical activity, arts, and music. Why? The human brain is born with well over a trillion connections. Synapses are being created all the time—especially in the early years—though half of them get shed by puberty. A child's experience determines which connections are shed and which are kept. This is why it's easier to learn to play an instrument or learn another language without a foreigner's accent before age ten. The more multi-sensory your child's environment, the more the possibility for learning is increased. That means finding ways to engage the eyes, ears, and whole body as much as possible.

Awareness of the key role you play is critical. It's also important to remember that your child's journey to learning—at all ages—is a wonderful discovery for both of you. It's a process that builds and deepens relationships. As each member of your family grows awareness of each other's individual and collective strengths, you all learn together how to best support one another with every challenge. As a result you'll create a healthier environment for your family as a whole.

> **MAKING IT REAL**
> *Next time you notice your child stuck, ask in a curious tone of voice, "I'm aware that you've been frustrated for a while doing your homework. What do you think is making it hard? What would help you right now?" Questions like these may help them identify what kinds of interferences are inhibiting their progress. Internal interferences are often more subtle and insidious, so questions like these can help you overcome them together.*

Why this matters today, more than ever

In our hyper-connected world, where soon every person on the planet will have a smartphone and network connection, the focus is shifting from making our kids "college-ready" to ensuring they are "life-ready." This comes from realizing that your child—like every child—learns and see things in their own unique way. The cookie cutter "one size fits all" approach society has been educating our children with will cease to work. No longer should it be about memorizing facts and figures, but rather helping your child use his or her talents and natural gifts to achieve life success.

By instilling self-awareness, and equipping your child with the knowledge of how he or she is smart, what's possible expands and grows their self-respect. This experience will also infuse a sense of self-motivation and deepen your child's capacity for learning, while fostering creativity, communication, collaboration, and critical thinking.

As a parent, mentor, and caregiver, you can also be your child's thinking partner as he or she faces challenges. A thinking partner evokes the child's own wisdom, rather than directing them what to do. As your child's thinking partner you believe your child has the innate ability to solve challenges and can use questions to help them figure out what they need. In doing so you recognize the innate value a child brings and support the development of it. You help them recognize what resources they need and with whom they need to collaborate to achieve success.

To be a thinking partner is to bring out their wisdom through questions. You might be surprised at how helping your child discover how he or she is smart unlocks your own capacity. You can be most effective in your role as a thinking partner by practicing the following mindset:

1 Truly "be" a partner on the journey; do this process with your child and not "to" them. Read the book, do the activities, and discover your own S.M.A.R.T. assets.

2 Be confident in your child's natural-born abilities.

3 Find ways to draw out and acknowledge your child's own experience. Ask questions such as, "How did you learn something so hard?"

4 Bridge the S.M.A.R.T. concepts to real-life challenges. Connect what you and your child are learning together with relevant issues such as homework, sports, and getting along with siblings.

As you do the activities in this book with your child, remember no one knows him or her better then you. Trust yourself. Trust your instincts. Listen. Observe. Ask questions. Participate.

When you embrace the concepts of *I Am Smart*, you join the legions of parents, educators, and other advocates around the world who are focused on creating healthy thinking and positive learning environments that encourage children to be their best.

CHAPTER TWO

The Four Guiding Principles

> "**Success is achieved by developing our strengths, not by eliminating our weaknesses.**"
> — Marilyn vos Savant

Our four guiding principles are based on an asset-focused approach to parenting. Instead of focusing on what isn't enough about your child (not smart enough, not articulate enough, not creative enough, not athletic enough), you help your child use his or her natural strengths to overcome limitations or difficulties. Imagine if your child were asked how she learned to spell those four words she got right on the test, then taught to use that same method on the sixteen others she misspelled? This is a very different approach than focusing on the sixteen she got wrong.

Each of the principles below will help you adopt this asset-focused approach and foster a learning mindset in your child. These principles also set the foundation for instilling self-awareness, self-trust, and self-confidence. When we focus on helping children understand what specific gifts each of them brings to the rest of us, we shift the perspective from worrying about what is wrong to wondering what could be possible.

1. Differences Are Resources, Not Disorders

Most of us sense that children learn in different ways. When a child doesn't measure up, we label their difference as everything from being difficult to having a disorder. If you hold Alexis and rock her while reading, she can pay attention for hours. But if you were to hold her brother Tony and try the same thing, he would be fidgeting the whole time. One is not better than the other; they are just different. Yet it is standard to judge children as if we all learn in the same way.

What if we switched this thinking and starting seeing learning disabilities as natural learning differences? What if we acknowledged we just don't all think and learn in the same way? We need to understand the nature of the different ways people use their minds. When we assess talent without considering the entire spectrum of intelligences, we mismatch education, careers, and jobs. The tragedy is that both our children and society at large lose out on the benefits of every child (and eventual adult) being able to realize their highest levels of performance, satisfaction, and competence.

Because we are all different, understanding the specific ways each one of us is uniquely wired becomes an important key to unlocking how we learn. If we accept that all who are different belong and are smart in their own way, then children from a young age can be taught and encouraged to stop judging, isolating, and bullying those who do not conform to some standardized norm.

Anyone who has ever had a child labeled with a disorder feels some reassurance when reading that British mystery author Agatha Christie refused to learn to write as a child, or that Albert Einstein did not speak until age seven. In fact, Einstein found schoolwork, especially math, incredibly difficult and was unable to express himself in written language. He was thought to be "simple-minded," until he was able to communicate by visualizing or writing rather than speaking.

Both Einstein and Christie struggled with standardized approaches in school. But somehow, found a way to develop their individual gifts. And there are thousand of other examples like this, people who today would be labeled as being difficult or having a disorder and who might even be medicated.

Too often this labeling and medicating deprives children of the help they need to understand and utilize their specific way of thinking. An asset-focused approach encourages you to consider how your child may have different learning strengths. In itself, learning how to use that difference well is a gift.

Think of ways to help your child celebrate his or her differences instead of being embarrassed by them. These can be physical differences (height, hair color, body type) or differences in the natural ways of express themselves (e.g. shy, talkative, physically reserved, or energetic).

2. Track Assets, Not Deficits

There is an established body of research in psychology, business, and education that supports the idea that it is better to track assets rather than deficits. Recall how your child first learned a basic skill, such as reaching for a cup. First the she reaches and gets Mommy's hair. Then air. Then Mommy's hand. Then air. Then cup. Then cup, cup, cup. In this moment, your infant's brain was actively learning how to track success and discard failure. The brain records each successful encounter with the cup and re-aims after each miss.

However, as a child gets older and particularly when he or she gets to school, this natural process is often reversed. We begin tracking failures. We pay attention to and test for right and wrong answers. As a consequence, we tend to de-skill our kids and stifle their natural passion to learn.

In a very real way, children are brighter when they begin their education than when they complete it. Brighter, as in more alert, more willing to experiment, to be wrong and laugh about it, more willing to risk, and reach for that cup. Very young children walk as if they belong on the earth, as if they are their own people, as if they trust their own minds. There is no gap between their true nature and their ability to express it.

Unintentionally, we damage children's curiosity and willingness to explore by focusing their attention on what does not work. We teach them to become aware of all the things that are wrong with them. The teacher marks how many words they get wrong on the spelling test, not how many they get right. They are told they are "weak in math." We grind an awareness of their mistakes into their brains. Thus, they take for granted what they do well and concentrate on their deficits. They come to distrust their mind's natural ability to learn.

This deficit focus is everywhere. It is so commonplace in our world that we think it's natural, but in reality, it's a very ineffective way for the human brain to work. Imagine for a moment that you keep depositing money in a savings account. But all you notice is the money that you don't have. You'd work even harder to make more money, which you'd put in the bank, then forget that you could withdraw it. You would always feel you were poor. This is a prime example of a deficit-focused mindset; awareness is the first step to changing this.

When Gallup asked parents, "What grade deserves the most time and attention: A, B, C, D, or F?" the vast majority said the F, with a mere seven percent saying the A.

Learn to track what your child does well, and use this to support him or her in areas where there are challenges.

3. See Mistakes As Experiments, Not Failures

In the attempt to standardize the way we measure children's learning, we give them the message that the right answer is more important than experimenting. The latest research in the study of the human brain indicates that experience can actually help to reshape its structure. This is why every child should be encouraged to explore his or her world through experiences and experiments. Since learning is increased through experimentation, and this requires making mistakes, an environment that humiliates, judges, corrects, embarrasses, criticizes, or labels a child for errors is one that decreases capacity.

The optimum learning environment is one that starts where a child is competent and challenges him or her to stretch, but not strain or stress. It is natural for children to quest, to pit themselves against outer obstacles and inner demons. To help them, you have only to work with that quest in a way that minimizes the habits of doubt and judgment that prevent performing at full capacity.

An effective learning environment should also be fun, because play is the very essence of learning. It can be the play of ideas and concepts or imagination and dreams. Without it, children can lose their sense of wonder and feeling of belonging to the world.

For example, Gracie, age five, is making something out of paper and scotch tape as her mother cooks dinner. She has been at work quietly for at least twenty minutes. Now comes the moment when she sees if it can stand on its own. Down it crashes in record speed. "Oh no," says Gracie. If her mother just came over and helped, Gracie would not learn to trust her own abilities. Instead, her mother could ask, "What could you do to make it stronger?" The key is asking the right question, so Gracie can experiment until she finds success. On her own, Gracie then runs to the cupboard for cardboard to reinforce her structure. In ten more minutes, she has created a standing house. But most importantly she has learned to trust her own learning process.
When children think of mistakes as failures, they become afraid to try new things. When they see mistakes as experiments, they are able to persist at something in order to reach their goal. They engage all their thinking in how it could be done differently.

The brain cannot learn if it is afraid to make a mistake; it simply shuts down. Help your child see mistakes as experiments for growth and learning, rather than failures.

4. Learn From the Inside Out As Well As the Outside In

The word "educate" comes either from the Latin educare, which means to instruct, as in training horses; or from educere, which means to lead forth that which is within. For the past 300 years, most schools and parents have been instructing from the outside in. We decide what children should learn and how they should learn it; we determine how long it should take, and evaluate how well it has been learned. We dismiss rather than foster children's own self-awareness of what works best for them and what is most important to them. They become adults who don't trust their own judgment, and need someone on the outside to determine the direction their life should take. No wonder young adults are so lost and can so easily get caught up in peer pressure! We have trained them to look outside themselves for the answers to challenges.

Inside-out learning requires something different from parents and teachers. As author Timothy Gallwey explains, "Most of us are more committed to teaching than to seeing someone else learn. Our ideas of teaching may come from the past and involve instilling judgment, doubt, and fear. Learning happens in an atmosphere of experimentation and self-correction, where the relationship between the student and his or her potential is protected."

Instead of directing from the outside in, learning from the inside out means helping children overcome obstacles that stand in the way of their doing quality work. They have to be guided to take responsibility for solving their own problems. For example, what if your child is required to turn in her homework every day. Every night, you ask, "Did you finish your homework? Make sure you turn it in." This works fine when you ask every single night, but what about the times you travel for work and the homework doesn't get turned in? What if, instead, you invite your child to come up with a reminder that puts him or her in charge of completing the homework and bringing it to school? Elizabeth, age eight, when asked to come up with her own solution, had the idea to put a reminder sticky note on her bathroom mirror. She had been actively engaged to finding the solution to her challenge.

Each time we help children learn from the inside out we are sending them the message that we respect their natural intelligence and capacity to master challenges. Those messages will build children's self-respect and confidence in their own assets.

Look for ways to empower your child's self-trust and let him or her experiment with different solutions to overcome challenges.

SMART Parenting Principles

Differences are resources, not disorders:	Track assets, not deficits:	See mistakes as experiments, not failures:	Learn from the inside out, as well as the outside in:
Every child thinks and learns differently. We must respect and honor those differences, and discover how to use them to learn and overcome challenges.	The more you focus on your children's assets-Successes, Mind Patterns, Attractions and Interests, Resources, and Thinking Talents—the more confident they will become, and the more they will be able to use what they learn to achieve success.	Experience is a great teacher. We all make mistakes, but rather than dwell on them, consider them opportunities for growth and learning.	Teaching children to follow their internal motivation to learn how they learn is at least as important as filling them with facts and information.

CHAPTER THREE

S.M.A.R.T: The Power of Thinking Differences

"Strength lies in differences, not in similarities."
— Stephen R. Covey

Recognizing your child's assets does not require that you become a different or better parent, merely that you shift what you are paying attention to. Rather than worrying that your child won't measure up to the other kids, won't get into the best school, won't do well on the test, you begin to look at what he or she does do well.

It is important to understand that recognizing assets is not the same as praising or complimenting. Praising is what you do to make another person feel good, whereas recognizing is noticing what is already there and being curious about how it can best be utilized and developed. A father, when shown his seven-year-old daughter's drawing says, "Oh that's beautiful; it should go in a museum." That is giving praise, and doesn't lead to learning or growth. On the other hand, if he were to ask her questions about what made it fun, what part she liked the best, and what she learned while she was drawing it, he would be helping her recognize her own assets.

Using this approach does not mean coddling children or ignoring their difficulties either. Rather, what's required is asking yourself: "How can I help my child use what's right to overcome what's wrong?" This is more like solving a riddle than trying to crack a problem. It's more like standing in front of your refrigerator and wondering how you can make the best meal out of the ingredients you already have, rather than following a set recipe and having to go to the store to buy new ingredients.

Through our process, we help you identify what your child's unique assets are by exploring the five categories of S.M.A.R.T. These are:

- **Successes:** How can successes of the past help a child in the future? When children identify their successes, along with the traits and formula they used to make them happen, they can then transfer this understanding to overcome challenges.

- **Mind Patterns:** What is the order of information that the brain needs to learn and communicate most effectively? What helps children naturally focus, explore, and be creative: Visual, auditory, or hands-on learning and communicating?

- **Attractions and Interests:** What are the ongoing things a child is passionate about? Look at how children light up when talking about something they love.

- **Resources:** What are the people, places, and things available to support a child? If children are aware of the support and resources that help them succeed, they'll feel more confident in a wide variety of situations.

- **Thinking Talents:** What are the natural ways of thinking that energize a child and makes him or her unique? Core to who children are, identifying these talents will help them excel and approach challenges effectively.

In the next section, we'll explore each asset category in detail. You'll be given a set of tools, questions to explore, and family activities to do together. As you go through each one, make notes about your child's assets in each of these areas. This information will be incorporated into their Smart Passport as a guide to help your child track his or her gifts and strengths.

> *"Every child has a unique way of being smart: particular talents, strengths, and conditions that are natural to follow when he or she learns. Every child has capacities that, when used effectively, can become a fulfilling, purposeful and joyful contribution to the world."*
>
> —Dawna Markova, Ph.D.

WHERE TO START?

1: Go through each of the S.M.A.R.T. categories with your child found in Part 2.

2: Get a notebook or journal and record your child's S.M.A.R.T. assets in each area. This becomes his or her personalized Smart Passport, documenting the different ways your child is naturally gifted, and the best ways to learn and excel. Review and add to the guide at regular intervals, tracking changes as your child grows.

3: You can also go online to www.smart-wired.com to access our interactive parenting app. Here you can input all your child's information on a secure database—one that can be easily updated by you or your child. Your child's profile can be viewed online, or printed and given to teachers, coaches, mentors, and others who have a relationship and could benefit from knowing what brings out your child's best.

PART 2:

THE SMART PARENTING PROCESS:
HOW TO RECOGNIZE AND DEVELOP THINKING DIFFERENCES

"We are all so different largely because we have different combinations of intelligences. If we recognize this, I think we will have at least a better chance of dealing appropriately with the many problems that we face in the world."
—Howard Gardner

CHAPTER FOUR

Successes:
Identify And Track
What Works

> "We need to accept that we won't always make the right decisions, that we'll screw up royally sometimes—understanding that failure is not the opposite of success, it's part of success."
>
> —Arianna Huffington

For most of us, we can easily and fluently list our failures in great detail. But for some reason our successes are harder to call out. Often, we keep a list of our children's perceived deficits that we worry will develop into adult flaws. Olivia never stands up for herself; I'm afraid she'll never learn to speak up. Tanya doesn't fit in. Rodrigo is too sensitive. Max is hyperactive and unfocused.

Tracking successes may be as easy as giving these worries an ending with possibilities: Olivia speaks up when her mom forgets to pack her favorite lunch as promised. That's a success. Tommy was frustrated, but last Tuesday he went out and threw rocks into a pond until his anger subsided. He was successful in directing his frustration and overcoming it instead of having a meltdown. That's a success. Max arranged all of his baseball cards in a suitcase; then he exchanged them for a skateboard.

He was successful at organizing and trading what he no longer wanted for something he did.

Tracking successes means recognizing what your child does right, does well, and does effectively. Taking pause to help children see what they did to make this success happen will help them uncover their innate success formula. This formula can then be applied to areas of learning where they are challenged.

> *"Everyone has their unique formula for success in their life. When you help your child recognize what their formula is, they'll know what to do to overcome challenges in school, relationships, and all areas of life."*
>
> —Dawna Markova, Ph.D.

S	M	A	R	T
Successes	Mind Patterns	Attractions and Interests	Resources	Thinking Talents
How can successes of the past help a child in the future?	What is the order of information that the brain needs to most effectively think, learn, and communicate?	What are the ongoing things a child is passionate about?	What are the people, places, and things available to support a child?	What are the natural ways of thinking that energize a child and make him or her unique?

WHERE TO START?

Identify your child's success formula.
Ask your child to think about one success he or she has had (what they're good and even great at). It could be from school, with family or friends, in sports, or even in playtime.
- *How do they know when something is a success?*
- *Have them act out, draw, write, or talk about this success.*

- *Explore with them the qualities they used to make this success happen.*
- *At night, have them share three things that went right during the day.*
- *Point out any of the success qualities they talk about to reinforce how these helped them.*

The following graphic depicts some different areas of life where you and your child can explore his or her successes.

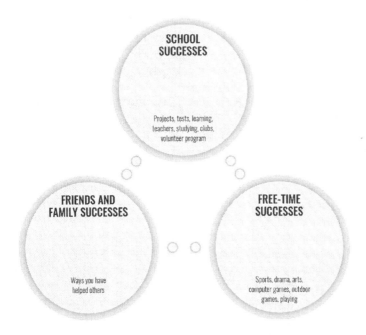

Here are some suggested "Success qualities" to help you as you both go through the exercise. It helps to think about what went into the success, so your child can apply that knowledge when they encounter something that's hard for them or they feel stuck.

- *Practiced*
- *Had strong goal/purpose*
- *Was prepared*
- *Thought creatively*
- *Learned from mistakes*
- *Overcame challenges*
- *Had courage*
- *Stuck to it*
- *Took risks*

2: ***Track and record what you both discover.*** This is where you start the Smart Passport. Keep a running a list of the successes as they happen, circling any qualities that stand out. Remember to add to and review this list. You can use his or her birthday to remind yourself to record them. If Dave was born December 28th, make the 28th of every month the day you add Successes. For example Dave shared there was bullying going on at the playground, and he stood up for his friend Tom even though he was scared. His mother told him she was proud of his courage and they recorded this quality in his Smart Passport.

3: ***Encourage your child to practice and use his or her unique success formula.*** If you know what your child's successes are, how can you help them use these to overcome challenging situations? Begin by asking them:
- "What has worked for you in the past?"
- "What success quality can you use from your list to help you?"

The most important component in helping children use their success formula is asking the questions that will bring their awareness to what the conditions were in the past when they met a similar challenge, as well as what qualities they applied to overcome that challenge.

Robin, for example, did brilliantly in French but was having problems understanding Biology. Her Godmother asked her what it was that made Biology so difficult. Robin was quick to explain that her mind kept snagging on words she had never heard before. Her Godmother asked her how she had learned all the French words so well. Robin showed the flash cards she had made, and then the light bulb went off. She realized she could make similar flash cards for Biology. In a month, her Biology grade and self-confidence rapidly climbed.

Taylor, following her dad skiing, suddenly found herself on a black diamond run. Looking at the steep pitch, she told her dad she was too scared to go forward. Instead of the typical parenting comment of "Don't worry, you can do it," Taylor's dad asked her, "What did you do the last time you were really scared to get over your fear?" She remembered her ski teacher telling her to just sing and "take it one turn at a time." Applying this success formula helped Taylor get down the mountain and have fun doing it.

If a situation arises when your child cannot recall a successful experience, then you can ask if they know of anyone else who has ever succeeded in a similar circumstance. By inquiring into that pattern, and wondering together how to apply it to the current challenge, your child will get a sense of what to do.

SMART Family Practices

- Begin a "joint study" of the causes of positive events with your child. When he was studying for that math exam, what made it possible for him to get such a great score? What was it that made you feel so excited about what happened at work? What made it possible for your daughter to learn to play soccer so readily: was it watching someone else, or being told how to make a particular play before she had to do it? How did your kids resolve that fight instead of beating up on each other?

- Have "Family Focus" meals: Dinner can be a time when the entire family focuses attention on one person, asking questions about their latest hero or heroine, what activity has made them happiest that week, what three things went well, or how they've used their strengths to face a challenge.

CHAPTER FIVE

Mind Patterns: Identify How Your Child Best Uses Attention to Focus, Sort, and Imagine

"Each mind has its own method."
— Ralph Waldo Emerson

We know that kids need to be "paying" attention in order to learn, but most of us don't know that there are different kinds of attention and all are important for learning. We may notice that some children love doing hands-on projects, while others will always draw or take notes when given a choice. Why does Kendall love to hold onto something when she is reading and Jordan always wants to listen to music while doing her homework? Too often, when a child cannot learn something, we rarely step back and ask "why?" or notice how they are being taught. We just assume there is something wrong. But the truth is every mind just works differently. It's through understanding these differences that we can help our children discover new ways to excel at learning and communicating.

The notion that we use different "operating systems" to learn has been at the center of our work for the last fifty years. Dawna uncovered it in the 1970's while working as a graduate student at Columbia and teaching in Harlem. Collaborating with researcher E. Roy John at NYU, who was measuring certain brain wave frequencies associated with general psychological processes, she was searching for effective reading methods to use with her students. As she saw them struggling to learn, she wanted to investigate what would work best to teach them: by sight, phonics, or a more hands-on approach. As E. Roy John had originated a field of study called Neurometrics, which used a computer and an EEG to monitor what was going in the brain while a person was thinking, she brought several children to his lab and connected them to the equipment. Her observations were fascinating. When Jack looked at written information, his brain produced more beta waves, indicating he was concentrating. But when she gave Julie the same information, her brain produced more alpha waves, which indicated a pondering state. Then, when the same visual information was presented to Jason, his brain produced more theta waves, a very spaced-out and imagining state.

What Dawna came to conclude was two-fold. First, input from the outside caused the children's brain to shift from focused attention to a daydream or creative state. Their different states of attention were being produced by the different kinds of input they were exposed to. And second, there is no single way of "paying attention." The brain uses all three states to learn and think.

Through this and other experiences in her work and research, she became convinced that the question was not, "Are children smart?" but rather, "HOW are they smart?" This awareness led her to create a system for understanding our differences in thinking, learning, and communicating, called Mind Patterns.

Giving attention to attention

In order to recognize how your child learns most effectively, it's important to understand the three states of attention our brains use.

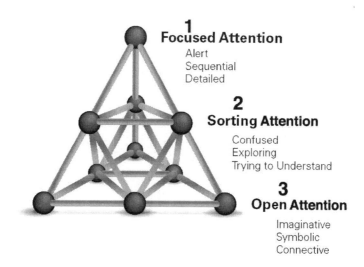

Focused attention. When we concentrate, our brains produce more beta waves. In this state, we are focused outward, are the most linear and sequential, and have the most mental stamina.

Sorting attention. When we are curious, even confused, our brains produce more alpha waves. This is where we are paying attention both to the external world and to ourselves.

Open attention. When we "space out" or daydream, our brains are producing more theta waves. This is where we are most imaginative, receptive, creative and sensitive.

When we use each of these states of attention, important steps in the learning process are occurring in our brains. Unfortunately, most of us have been led to believe that learning only occurs when we are in Focused attention: the alert, outward-focused beta mode. Incorrectly, we assume that Sorting attention (when our brains "understand" something), and Open attention (when new ideas are generated) are useless wastes of time.

For example, when Penn's teacher asks him a question and he looks away, saying nothing, it does not necessarily mean that he isn't paying attention. It may mean that his brain is digesting what he's heard and "thinking" about it with Sorting attention. Kendall, when writing a story, may stare out the window. It doesn't mean she's zoned out, merely that she is imagining, using Open attention. Concentrating, organizing, wondering, imagining, deciding, and expressing are all different parts of learning.

To figure our your Mind Pattern, you need to know about the 3 inputs that spark your brain.		
Auditory Thinking	**Kinesthetic Thinking**	**Visual Thinking**
• Listening • Telling • Discussing • Singing • Talking	• Doing • Moving • Feeling • Making Things	• Looking • Watching • Reading • Showing • Observing • Writing

Different external inputs—auditory, kinesthetic, or visual—trigger different ways of paying attention in different children. Mind Patterns are the natural sequence in which your child's mind processes information using the three sensory triggers. In her research, Dawna identified six possible Mind Pattern combinations. The more you and your child understand his or her Mind Pattern, the easier learning will become.

VAK PATTERN: Visual, Auditory and Kinesthetic			
V1	👁	Focused Thinking	Visual to Trigger Concentration
A2	👂	Sorting Thinking	Auditory to Trigger Concentration
K3	✋	Open Thinking	Kinesthetic to Trigger Concentration

VKA PATTERN: Visual, Kinesthetic and Auditory			
V1	👁	Focused Thinking	Visual to Trigger Concentration
K2	✋	Sorting Thinking	Kinesthetic to Trigger Concentration
A3	👂	Open Thinking	Auditory to Trigger Concentration

KAV PATTERN: Kinesthetic, Auditory and Visual			
K1	✋	Focused Thinking	Kinesthetic to Trigger Concentration
A2	👂	Sorting Thinking	Auditory to Trigger Concentration
V3	👁	Open Thinking	Visual to Trigger Concentration

KVA PATTERN: Kinesthetic, Visual and Auditory			
K1	✋	Focused Thinking	Kinesthetic to Trigger Concentration
V2	👁	Sorting Thinking	Visual to Trigger Concentration
A3	👂	Open Thinking	Auditory to Trigger Concentration

AVK PATTERN: Auditory, Visual and Kinesthetic			
A1	👂	Focused Thinking	Auditory to Trigger Concentration
V2	👁	Sorting Thinking	Visual to Trigger Concentration
K3	✋	Open Thinking	Kinesthetic to Trigger Concentration

AKV PATTERN: Auditory, Kinesthetic and Visual			
A1	👂	Focused Thinking	Auditory to Trigger Concentration
K2	✋	Sorting Thinking	Kinesthetic to Trigger Concentration
V3	👁	Open Thinking	Visual to Trigger Concentration

For example, playing with something in his hands and moving around helps Jerome focus and concentrate. Writing it down helps Gabriella focus. Talking about it first helps Suzanne focus. All three children are in a state of focused attention. All three are learning. They just each need a different input to help them do that.

To understand what he is learning, Jerome stares into space, doodles, or draws on his iPad. Gabriella tells stories or says, "Well, it's kind of like sand going through your fingers." Suzanne jiggles her foot. All three children's brains are now in Sorting attention, but each is using a different way to process and sort through information.

When Jerome comes to a deep place of understanding, he'll be quiet for quite some time and then ask a big wide question. Gabriella will get absolutely still and feel as if she is floating off into space, and Suzanne will stare out the window and see movies in her mind. Different triggers are helping all three children's brains into Open attention, producing more theta waves as they innovate and imagine.

WHERE TO START?

1: *Identify the unique way your child's mind uses these different Mind Patterns.* Go through the discovery process with your child on the next few pages to identify his or her Mind Pattern.

It's important to note: this discovery process has been designed to increase your awareness of how the three triggers create different states of attention. When you complete the process with your child, you can reference the corresponding Mind Pattern profiles, which will give you the detailed description and characteristics for that pattern. This information is meant to increase your curiosity and awareness of how your child is affected by different experiences, and how he or she can be most effective with others. It does not describe personality, although many of the characteristics of a person's Mind Pattern are often incorrectly attributed to that. It also is not related to gender. As you read the different descriptions, please be aware that any single characteristic may not be one hundred percent true for your child—what is significant is the overall pattern, and what works best for your child to learn and communicate.

The descriptions are based on more than forty years of research and data collected from tens of thousands of people who have used this material. If over time, the Mind Pattern that your child selected does not seem to fit, you may want to read through the other patterns and see if another is more accurate. Some people recognize their child's pattern immediately. Others need to observe their child in this new way over time, until they find an accurate fit. What is most important is that you continue to increase your curiosity about the unique and amazing ways that your child's mind works.

Mind Pattern Discovery

To identify your child's Mind Pattern, simply read the descriptions on the following "cards" which describe what triggers your child into a Focused state of attention. Choose whichever of the three cards (V1, K1, or A1) sounds most like your child. Then follow the instructions and decide between the two available card options to narrow down their trigger for Open attention, and you'll be guided to their corresponding Mind Pattern description.

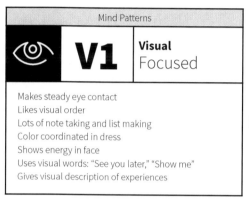

Mind Patterns	
👁 **V1**	**Visual** Focused

Makes steady eye contact
Likes visual order
Lots of note taking and list making
Color coordinated in dress
Shows energy in face
Uses visual words: "See you later," "Show me"
Gives visual description of experiences

Next Step:
On the following page...

Read K3 or A3 and see which is more true for your child.

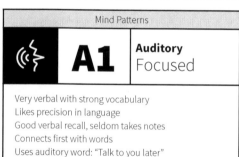

Mind Patterns	
🗣 **A1**	**Auditory** Focused

Very verbal with strong vocabulary
Likes precision in language
Good verbal recall, seldom takes notes
Connects first with words
Uses auditory word: "Talk to you later"

Read K3 or V3 and see which is more true for your child.

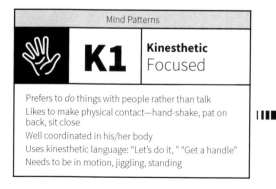

Mind Patterns	
✋ **K1**	**Kinesthetic** Focused

Prefers to *do* things with people rather than talk
Likes to make physical contact—hand-shake, pat on back, sit close
Well coordinated in his/her body
Uses kinesthetic language: "Let's do it, " "Get a handle"
Needs to be in motion, jiggling, standing

Read V3 or A3 and see which is more true for your child.

Mind Patterns	
K3	**Kinesthetic** Open

Can sit still without moving for long time periods of time
Shy about touch
Easily forgets how to do something
Tends to be awkward physically
Rarely talks about action, sports, or experiences

If you chose A1 and K3 see the AVK profile on page 45.

If you chose V1 and K3, see the VAK profile on page 49.

Mind Patterns	
V3	**Visual** Open

Eye shy, looks away or down frequently
Little or no note taking
Easily forgets what things look like
Concerned more with comfort rather than appearance in clothing
Rarely describes how something looks
Prefers talking or doing to writing
Too many visual details or extensive reading spaces him/her out

If you chose A1 and V3 see the AKV profile on page 46.

If you chose K1 and V3, see the KAV profile on page 47.

Mind Patterns	
A3	**Kinesthetic** Open

May take longer to speak, pauses between thoughts
Easily distracted by loud noises
Highly sensitive to voice tone, sarcasm
Speaks more in questions than statements
Too much listening and long explanations spaces him/her out
Easily forgets what you say

If you chose K1 and A3 see the KVA profile on page 48.

If you chose V1 and A3, see the VKA profile on page 50.

Note: If you read the profile suggested and it doesn't match the general characteristics of your child, read the other profiles and see if there is a better fit.

The Six Mind Pattern Profiles

Use the information in the profiles below to create an environment that best supports how your child learns, communicates, and overcomes challenges.

AVK PATTERN: Auditory, Visual and Kinesthetic			
A1	👂	Focused Thinking	**Auditory** to Trigger Concentration
V2	👁	Sorting Thinking	**Visual** to Trigger Concentration
K3	✋	Open Thinking	**Kinesthetic** to Trigger Concentration

FUN FACTS:
- AVK's love to talk and debate with others. They make great reporters, professors, and communicators.
- Your child needs to talk for his or her brain to focus and pay attention.
- Reading/drawing/doodling will help your child's brain sort and understand.
- Moving and doing hands-on activities is where your child's brain is the most sensitive and imaginative.

Your child learns best by hearing and discussing. The sorting state is triggered when your child reads or sees the visual details of the information. Finally, to trigger a more open "imaginative state," your child prefers to learn with pictures and diagrams that are simple.

Communication: Your child has a good vocabulary and is a strong and energetic speaker (he or she will make statements rather than ask questions). AVK children can easily write about what they have heard. Writing short paragraphs and drawing diagrams comes easily. You'll notice your child might not prefer to do physical activities with many other people, and instead prefer individual sports vs. being on a team.

Challenges: Your child may have a tendency to excitedly interrupt others, boss people verbally, or sound like a know-it-all. Your child may have trouble understanding things if he or she cannot see a diagram, chart, or a picture of what someone wants him/her to do. If involved in too many physical tasks or playing sports competitively, he or she can become shy.

AKV PATTERN: Auditory, Kinesthetic and Visual			
A1	🗣	Focused Thinking	**Auditory** to Trigger Concentration
K2	✋	Sorting Thinking	**Kinesthetic** to Trigger Concentration
V3	👁	Open Thinking	**Visual** to Trigger Concentration

FUN FACTS:
- AKV's love to talk and inspire others; they make great coaches, politicians, and TV/radio hosts.
- Your child needs to talk for his or her brain to focus and pay attention.
- Moving and doing hands-on activities helps your child's brain sort and understand.
- Reading/drawing/doodling is where your child's brain is the most sensitive and imaginative.

Your child learns best by hearing and talking first. The sorting state is triggered by doing physical things or a hand's-on approach—experiential learning helps your child remember things. Finally, to trigger a more open "imaginative state," your child prefers to learn with pictures and diagrams that are simple.

Communication: Your child has a good vocabulary and is a strong and energetic speaker (he or she will usually talk in statements rather than ask questions). Your child will use his or her hands and like to move while speaking. Your child prefers not to write long e-mails or notes.

Challenges: Your child can have a tendency to excitedly interrupt others, boss people verbally, or sound like a know-it-all. He or she might get criticized for fidgeting or moving around a lot. Too much visual information will space him/her out.

KAV PATTERN: Kinesthetic, Auditory and Visual			
K1	✋	Focused Thinking	**Kinesthetic** to Trigger Concentration
A2	🗣	Sorting Thinking	**Auditory** to Trigger Concentration
V3	👁	Open Thinking	**Visual** to Trigger Concentration

FUN FACTS:
- KAV's are great doers and love to build and fix things. They make great athletes, explorers, and engineers.
- Your child needs to move and have hands-on experiences for his or her brain to focus and pay attention.
- Talking will help your child's brain sort and understand.
- Writing/drawing and reading is where your child's brain is the most sensitive and imaginative.

Your child learns best by first doing something. Discussing what has just been taught triggers the "sorting" state. Finally, to trigger a more open "imaginative" state, your child should look at images and diagrams.

Communication: Your child likes to do things as he or she talks. They enjoy talking about personal experiences and are skilled at explaining physical tasks. They prefer not to write long letters or emails.

Challenges: It is hard for your child to sit still for long periods. Your child can get criticized for going on and on verbally, without getting to the point. Long reading and writing assignments can be difficult.

KVA PATTERN: Kinesthetic, Visual and Auditory

K1	✋	Focused Thinking	**Kinesthetic** to Trigger Concentration
V2	👁	Sorting Thinking	**Visual** to Trigger Concentration
A3	🗣	Open Thinking	**Auditory** to Trigger Concentration

FUN FACTS:
- KVA's love nature, physical activity, and are doers. They make great doctors, athletes, and architects.
- Your child needs to move and have hands-on experiences for his or her brain to focus and pay attention.
- Reading/drawing/doodling will help your child's brain sort and understand.
- Talking and listening is when your child's brain is the most sensitive and imaginative.

Your child learns best by first doing something. The sorting state gets triggered when your child reads or can see the details of what he or she is trying to learn. Writing notes in diagrams or using pictures will help them remember facts. To trigger the "imaginative" state, your child prefers talking one-on-one or in small groups.

Communication: Your child prefers to do things as he or she talks. It helps for them to take notes and write about what they're hearing; talking is easiest while your child is doing something else simultaneously. Your child might be considered "shy" in class unless he or she can read from notes or move around.

Challenges: It may be difficult to listen to long lectures, unless your child can move around and see visuals. It's hard for your child when someone explains something without showing them. They may have trouble if they cannot see a diagram, chart, or picture of what someone is talking about. It's often hard to "recall" what someone said. Public speaking or debating can be difficult.

VAK PATTERN: Visual, Auditory and Kinesthetic			
V1	👁	Focused Thinking	**Visual** to Trigger Concentration
A2	🗣	Sorting Thinking	**Auditory** to Trigger Concentration
K3	✋	Open Thinking	**Kinesthetic** to Trigger Concentration

FUN FACTS:
- VAK's love to tell stories and teach things. They make great teachers, writers, and community leaders.
- Your child needs to see and write for his or her brain to focus and pay attention.
- Talking through something will help your child's brain sort and understand.
- Moving and doing hands-on activities is where your child's brain is the most sensitive and imaginative.

Your child learns best by first reading and writing detailed notes. The sorting state gets triggered when your child discusses and talks about what he or she has just learned. Hands-on activities are harder to do but trigger the "imaginative" state.

Communication: Your child enjoys reading and finds writing long emails or notes easy. He or she enjoys talking about what they see and are skilled at showing and telling a story. Your child would prefer not to do physical activities publicly with many people.

Challenges: It can be difficult when someone explains something just by talking, without showing your child how to do it. Your child can get criticized for going on and on, without getting to the point. Your child will feel shy when he or she has to do forced physical activities or play sports competitively.

VKA PATTERN:		Visual, Kinesthetic and Auditory	
V1	👁	**Focused Thinking**	**Visual** to Trigger Concentration
K2	✋	**Sorting Thinking**	**Kinesthetic** to Trigger Concentration
A3	🗣	**Open Thinking**	**Auditory** to Trigger Concentration

FUN FACTS:
- VKA's love to work with others and make things beautiful and functional. They make great designers, writers, TV directors, and Web or app developers.
- Your child needs to see and write for his or her brain to focus and pay attention.
- Moving and hands-on experiences will help your child's brain sort and understand.
- Listening and talking is where your child's brain is the most sensitive and imaginative.

Your child learns best by first reading, seeing things done, and writing detailed notes. The sorting state gets triggered when your child does things hands-on. To trigger the "imaginative" state, your child prefers talking one-on-one or in small groups.

Communication: Your child prefers to write out how they feel (rather than talking about it). They can easily read and write long notes or emails. In order to feel comfortable speaking, your child needs to move. Often, they're a natural at sports that require visual focus, such as tennis. Your child might feel shy to speak up in class, unless he or she can read from notes or move around.

Challenges: It can be difficult when someone explains something just by talking, without showing your child how to do it. Your child finds it hard to learn something if he or she can't experience it. They might have trouble recalling what is said and public speaking or debating can be hard.

2: **Track and record what you both discover.** Take out your child's Smart Passport. Record not only his or her Mind Pattern, but also key insights you've observed into the best way he or she learns, communicates, and is challenged. What helps them focus, what do they need first? ("Visuals and reading and writing help me to focus"). What helps them sort and explore? ("Doing something physical helps me sort things out and think through problems"). Where are they the most sensitive? ("I find loud sounds or loud talking distracting or overwhelming.")

3: **Encourage your child to practice and use what they've learned about how their brain works best.** Help switch the thinking from "I can't do this," to "What does my brain need to learn this?" Review the tips in Chapter Ten on page 85 on how to best use your child's Mind Pattern to overcome challenges and learn something new.

SMART Family Practices

Have every family member go through the Mind Pattern discovery process and identify their own pattern. Create a family chart that lists each individual's pattern. Share and write out the best way to support each other when you get frustrated. Share the best way each person would like to communicate or how each one is most sensitive.

Our Family Communications Center

Each family member writes in the keys to his/her Mind Pattern.

Kinesthetic Visual Auditory	Kinesthetic Auditory Visual
K V A	**K A V**

Visual Kinesthetic Auditory	Visual Auditory Kinesthetic
V K A	**V A K**

Auditory Visual Kinesthetic	Auditory Kinesthetic Visual
A V K	**A K V**

Share: What's the best way to support you when you're frustrated?

Share: Who's the best person to help you figure something out?

CHAPTER SIX

Attractions and Interests: Identify and Motivate with What Your Child Naturally Loves to Do

> "Pay attention to the curiosities of a child; this is where the search for knowledge is freshest and most valuable."
> —Albert Einstein

One of the assets every person possesses but often takes for granted are the attractions and interests he or she has. What we all love and are drawn to is unique to us. Think for a moment about what kinds of activities and subjects your child has always been gravitated to. Does she love computers and all things electronic? Is he a stick and stone collector? Does she love insects? Does he love to play computer games? Does she draw and make things?

Eight-year-old Phineas, for example, has always loved music. When he was two, his father gave him a xylophone. His eyes lit up as he used the mallets on those keys, totally amazed that he could be making such sounds. For years, he and his mother ended the day with a song. Now he goes to sleep with his iPod, playing his favorite playlists, and is learning the drums.

Sixteen-year-old Mary spends her free time in her room with her nose buried in a book; she figures she has read at least three hundred novels. Meanwhile her sister Shelly is always outside—swimming, skiing, cycling, or skateboarding. Rosa loves to make things with her hands, spending her free time knitting, crocheting, making jewelry and pottery. Attractions and interests are often the very things children end up pursuing their whole life, and can be clues to their life path. In the book *Einstein Never Used Flashcards*, the authors point out that Einstein wasn't drilled in multiplication tables as a child. Rather, his parents paid attention to his side interests and gave him opportunities to explore them.

In recognizing your child's attractions and interests, you are tapping into his or her natural motivation. These become compass points that he or she can return to and call on when facing an unknown situation. When you know these points, you can use them to help your child for growth and learning.

So, how can you use your child's interests to learn something else he or she can draw on when challenged? Brian, age eleven, was an excellent swimmer but lacked confidence in every other area of his life. He walked around hunched over and spoke very little. His swimming coach decided to use him as an assistant to help with the beginning swimmers. Brian excelled at this—the young children followed him around as if he were Peter Pan. He stood tall. He began to relate everything to his love of swimming: he gave his oral English report on Florence Chadwick who swam across the English Channel; he began to think of handwriting as if it were the butterfly stroke and, with his coach's help, started to see going to school like training for the Olympics.

Maya was sixteen and outwardly very shy; she never spoke more than a necessary word or two to anyone. She would close herself in her room each day and read poetry for hours on end. One day, the school librarian said to her, "You know, Maya, you can't really love poetry." Maya nodded her head defiantly. The librarian said, "No you don't, because poetry is meant to be read aloud. If you really loved it, you'd find ways to read poetry so that others could hear it too." Maya went away and thought about the librarian's words. At her church's annual talent show, she sent a note to the minister asking if she could read some of her own poetry. When her turn came, she surprised everybody by reading with a fierce, vibrant voice. Maya Angelou won the contest and grew up to be the first African-American poet laureate of the United States.

> *"Children should not fail. If they do so, it is we who have not yet learned how to help them suceed."*
>
> —Dawna Markova, Ph.D.

What does your child love and have a passion for? What lights him or her up like nothing else? Particular hobbies and passions are invaluable learning tools.

WHERE TO START?

1: *Identify your child's attractions and interests.* Include everything you can think of, even the things with which you might not be especially thrilled, like an attraction to fire or fast cars. Consider both the activities that your child selects on their own, the games they make up, and the things they do when alone and not prompted. Also consider the activities you have offered to do with them that they have responded to positively, like cooking. Use your knowledge of their Mind Pattern by asking if they prefer to write out, act out, or tell you the things they love or that light them up.

Make sure you include everything, no matter how weird, wild, wonderful, big, secret, radical, scary, and strange—as you never know what that helps reveal.

2: ***Track and record what you both discover.*** Write down the list in your child's Smart Passport. Reading, poetry, dreaming, Star Wars, boxing, making music, skydiving, football, bugs, texting—make sure to record it all.

3: ***Encourage your child to practice and use what he or she loves to help motivate them.*** Ask your child what it is about the things they like that excite them? How can the exciting aspects help them in an area where they're bored or frustrated? John finds history boring but loves paintball. What about writing an essay on the history of paintball?

SMART Family practices

- Have each family member write out a list of how they use their free time. From the list, have each person star the things they truly love and circle what they find frustrating. Use this as a way to discuss exactly what each person loves, what they would like to have more time for, and how they could support each other better in creating time to pursue these interests.
- At dinner have each person answer: "What's your favorite activity of all time?" and "What have you always wanted to try and haven't yet?"

CHAPTER SEVEN

Resources: Identify and Succeed with People, Places, and Things that Bring Out Your Child's Best

> "One looks back with appreciation to the brilliant teachers, but with gratitude to those who touched our human feelings. The curriculum is so much necessary raw material, but warmth is the vital element for the growing plant and for the soul of the child."
>
> —Carl Jung

Other assets that are useful in bringing out the best in your child are the people, places, tools, and programs available in their environment. In other words, the Resources out in the world that he or she has access to. In order to identify your child's Resources, it's necessary for you to accept that even the most perfect parent with infinite free time couldn't meet all of a child's needs—nor are you meant to. "It takes a village to raise a child." What you can do is recognize where the Resources can be found within your child's world to make it possible for him or her to use them.

> *What does your child love and have a passion for? What lights him or her up like nothing else? Particular hobbies and passions are invaluable learning tools.*

Mark was a twelve-year-old boy who was about to get into trouble. His older brothers and most of the kids in his neighborhood were deep into drugs. His single mother worked day and night to support her family. Mark had no heroes. One day after school, a cousin invited him to the neighborhood Boys & Girls Club. Having nothing better to do, he reluctantly agreed. On the first afternoon, one of the volunteers offered to help with his homework. Then he asked Mark to join a Karate class. It was the first time in Mark's life he got to experience a positive, male guiding hand. For the rest of his school years, Mark returned to the Boys & Girls Club every afternoon. Then he joined the Marine Corps where he worked his way up to become a high-ranking leader as well as a hero to thousands of other young men and women.

Seven-year-old Sophie was bored at school and didn't think much of herself. One day, walking home from school, she passed a park where girls of all ages were dressed in costumes and practicing traditional Irish dances. She sat down and watched until they were done. The teacher approached Sophie as she was about to leave and invited her to come and join the class. Sophie discovered to her delight that dancing was an area in which she excelled. It turned out that the class was not only about dance, but also about learning the music, language, and crafts that were part of her Irish heritage. Each time she joined the class she felt like a tree finding its roots. She told her mother and sisters about what she was learning, and then one day, worked up enough courage to teach the other children in her class about Irish folk dancing.

Consider the following reflective questions—how do they apply to your child?

Resource	Question	Example
People	Who are the people that bring out the best in your child?	Miguel was going through a dark period until he spent time every day with his aunt Maria helping her cook. She was the one person in the world that made him laugh no matter what.
Environments	What is the environment that most helps your child concentrate? Sort things out? Come up with new ideas?	Harper came home from school very wound up. Spending a half hour in her room dancing to loud music calmed her down enough to focus on homework.
Places	What is missing for your child and what kind of person or place would help him or her find it?	After his parents were divorced, Lawrence spent every afternoon in the Boys & Girls Club playing basketball with a coach that really cared about him.
Classes/workshops	What could your child learn that would increase his or her self-confidence and self-trust?	Steffi had no friends in school. After taking a pottery class at the local YWCA, she realized that she could create beautiful things and no longer felt worthless.
Objects	What are the things that might assist your child directing his or her energy in a positive way?	Simon was small for his age and kept getting picked on in school. For his birthday he was given a drum. He spent hours pounding on it to vent his frustration and anger. Drumming became his release that enabled him to feel and act more confidently.

WHERE TO START?

1: ***Identify a time when your child was at his or her best.*** What Resources have helped your child overcome a limitation in the past? Have them tell a story about it, act, or draw it out.
- Notice things from the story: who was there? What were they doing? What objects or tools were being used? Where were they? What was the environment like?
- Ask your child to describe the people (parent, teacher, friend's parent, mentor, coach, brother/sister etc.), places (outside, school, library, field, beach, swimming pool, bedroom etc.), and things (art supplies, musical instruments, wood blocks, Legos, computers, tablets, etc.) that helped them in different ways, along with "how" they helped them.

2: ***Track and record what you both discover.*** Make a list in the Smart Passport. Get your child to be as specific as possible (e.g. "soccer" as opposed to just "sports," "My dad helps me study while by brother helps me when I'm confused," "Moving helps me create while playing guitar helps me relax.")

3: ***Encourage your child to use these Resources to help him or her succeed.*** How can the places, people, and things they love help them in all areas of their life?

SMART Family Practices
- ***Develop the skill of self-evaluation***, which places the focus on how he or she is learning rather than on grades or other assessments that come from the outside. One way to do this is to regularly ask open-ended questions that help him or her to recognize, utilize, and develop her assets. Open-ended questions are questions that you wouldn't know the answer to unless your child told you, questions that are asked with simple, genuine curiosity. Some of these questions might be, "What do you like most about the work you produced?" "What are you most proud of?" "What was the hardest part?" "When did you get stuck?"

"How did you help yourself get unstuck?" "How did you have fun?"
- **Create a "satisfaction stop."** Children (and us parents) run from one thing on the list to the next without ever stopping to learn and appreciate the experience and accomplishments completed. You can help your child create frequent and brief satisfaction stops. By taking two minutes to pause and celebrate, you help deepen the experience. For example, at the end of hard math homework, you can ask your child, "What do you like most about what you just did?" After he shares his thoughts, ask how he would like to celebrate (like listening to a song, or doing a victory dance—in short, doing something he loves).
- **Find fun ways to track what your child is learning.** Get a map of the world and flag all the places your child knows something about with her favorite color marking the places she wants to visit. Make a timeline of the growing list of people he admires. Make a compilation of all the books he's read or the songs she can play on the piano.

CHAPTER EIGHT:

Thinking Talents: Identify and Develop the Ways Your Child Thinks that Makes Him or Her Unique

> "Don't ask yourself what the world needs; ask yourself what makes you come alive. And then go do that. Because what the world needs is people who have come alive."
>
> –Howard Thurman

Typically, when you hear the word "talented," your mind goes to music or sports. But in fact, we all have unique thinking talents, special mental capacities that each individual is born with. Thinking Talents are the natural ways your child approaches challenges with a certain excellence that increase his or her mental energy. Rather than being bored, burned out or drained, a child is energized when using these ways of thinking. These talents don't have to be taught, but they can be developed. Our job as parents is to recognize them, help our children recognize them, and use them to work around the things they're not naturally good at. Thinking Talents are so intrinsic that if they were to disappear your child would be nearly unrecognizable to you.

When children are young, they may have many Thinking Talents. As they get older, the brain begins to follow certain habitual pathways. A few become like superhighways. The ones they don't use as much are shut down. Extensive research on excellence with over two million people by the Gallup organization shows that by the time we are adults, most of us use somewhere in the range four to six Thinking Talents.

Why knowing your child's Thinking Talents is important
- It enables them to use their minds in ways that are natural to them.
- It increases their ability to learn and grow.
- It helps us understand why we all think differently and how to respect those differences.

In the next few pages, you'll have the opportunity to identify your child's Thinking Talents by reading through each of the twenty-four talents shown. Keep in mind as you go through each one that Thinking Talents:

- *Are innate ways of thinking.* That is, your child will naturally be really good at thinking this way, even if they've never had any specific training. They'll always prefer to use them when they think about challenges.

- *Give your child energy.* Your child gets joy and energy from using these Thinking Talents; they can think this way for long periods without getting burned out.

Understanding these two aspects will help you distinguish Thinking Talents from skills, personality traits, and other capacities.

Thinking Talents in action
We found that it wasn't enough for parents just to understand what their child's Thinking Talents were. Drawing on powerful research conducted by renowned learning specialist Ned Hermann, we arranged the Thinking Talents into four broad categories to make them easier to apply to every day situations. The four categories are: Analytic, Procedural, Relational, and Innovative. In the same way that an orchestra is divided into four

groups of similar instruments, these four quadrants represent a different way of thinking through problems. By the end of this chapter, you'll have the tools to identify your child's Thinking Talents and map them accordingly.

Twelve-year-old Trent had the Thinking Talent of "Precision;" he was extremely procedural even at such a young age. Trent started to complain to his father (his parents were divorced) how Mom was late all the time to pick him up or get him to soccer, so he asked to come live at his Dad's house. Even though his father wanted to have more time with Trent he knew his ex-wife would be hurt by their son's request.

She sat down with him and explored their thinking differences. When his ex saw the map, she saw how Procedural thinking—being on time, planning, and responsibility—was Trent's strength. On the other hand, her talents were mostly in the Relational quadrant. She was so focused on making sure he was emotionally well and happy, that she overlooked his frustration with her. Trent was mistaking her behavior of never being on time as not caring for him. Together they drew up a "promise sheet" and put it on the fridge. She promised to be very aware of time, and he promised to talk about his feelings more.

Eight-year-old Nicola was clingy and didn't want to go to school. Her mother noticed that she responded positively when challenged to be first at something. When she brought Nicola to school one day, she whispered a competitive challenge in her ear as she gave her a hug, "If you can be the first one into class, the first to raise your hand, and the first one out at lunchtime, I'll give you fourteen hugs and kisses when I pick you up in the afternoon." Spurred forward by her natural Thinking Talent of "Wanting to Win," Nicola was off like a shot.

Kenneth, age eight, began to have nightmares and couldn't sleep through the night. From working through our process, his father recognized Kenneth's Thinking Talent of "Storytelling." One night after tucking Kenneth into bed, his father said, "Let's turn things around. You tell me a story tonight. Make sure it starts out really scary but has a great ending." Kenneth told a story about a young wizard who had to fight to protect the queen of the land. The wizard gathered magical creatures to surround the queen's castle so she would be safe. The wizard became the hero for saving the queen. Kenneth slept easy that night. His parents were so delighted that each night, one of them would ask him to tell scary stories with positive endings. Without realizing it, Kenneth was using his stories to work through When his own fears.

WHERE TO START?

1: *Identify and Map Your child's Thinking Talents.* Go through and read the description on each of the following Thinking Talents. You will see that each Thinking Talent has a label at the bottom that reads "Always-Sometimes-Never." We suggest you take a piece of paper and create three columns with these labels. Write the talents in the appropriate columns. "This ALWAYS gives him or her energy." "This SOMETIMES gives him or her energy." "This NEVER gives him or her energy."

Once you have placed all of the talents into one of the three categories, go to the "ALWAYS" group and edit it down to the four to six strongest talents. If you have more than six, consider which ones have always been true for your child; eliminate those that aren't quite as strong. If you have fewer than four, go to the "SOMETIMES" group and add the strongest ones there to the "ALWAYS" group until you have at least four. You may find one or more talents in your child's "ALWAYS" group that you think of as irrelevant, but if it fits the above criteria, please consider it a Thinking Talent anyway. The four to six cards remaining in the "ALWAYS" group will most accurately describe what you consider to be your child's strongest Thinking Talents.

> *Don't worry, there is no way you can be wrong with this process. As your awareness of your child's Thinking Talents increases, you may notice things about them you hadn't noticed, so you may need to reconsider some of the choices. As your understanding grows, these can always be changed.*

THINKING TALENTS
Connection

"How is this part of something larger?"

Loves to connect people and/or ideas; sees the relationship between things and/or people; perceives how one thing is part of something larger.

THINKING TALENTS
Enrolling

"How can I relate to this new person?"

Enjoys challenge of meeting new people and getting in their good graces; enjoys developing rapport, breaking the ice, making a new connection, then moving on.

THINKING TALENTS
Feeling for Others

"What are people feeling now?"

Senses emotions in those nearby; shares their perspective in order to understand their choices; hears the unvoiced questions; anticipates others' needs.

THINKING TALENTS
Fixing It

"What's the solution to this problem?"

Energized by breakdowns; loves to identify what's wrong and repair it, or anticipate what might go wrong and avert it. Enjoys rescuing and saving something.

THINKING TALENTS

Get to Action

"What can I do right now?"

Impatient for action rather than contemplation. Must make something happen.

THINKING TALENTS

Goal Setting

"What can I accomplish today?"

The daily drive to accomplish something and meet a goal. Every day starts at 0 and must achieve something tangible. There is a perpetual whisper of discontent.

THINKING TALENTS

Humor

"What is amusing about this?"

Enjoys finding the humor in situations. Can lighten tense moments and puts self and others at ease with laughter.

THINKING TALENTS

Innovation

"How can this be done differently?"

Loves to create new processes or products; easily bored with routine. Energized by never having done it before.

THINKING TALENTS

Loving Ideas

"What's a thrilling idea or theory to explain this?"

Searches for concepts to explain things; loves theories; derives jolt of energy from a new idea.

THINKING TALENTS

Love of Learning

"What can I learn next?"

Drawn always to the process of learning more than the content; energized by the journey from ignorance to competence. The outcome is less important than what is learned.

THINKING TALENTS

Making Order

"How can I align all these different variables?"

Enjoys managing and aligning many variables into the best configuration; jumps into confusion and devises new options; organizes what's messy.

THINKING TALENTS

Mentoring

"What can help others grow?"

Sees potential in others; every person is a work in progress; goal is to help others achieve success; searches for signs of growth in others.

THINKING TALENTS
Optimism

"What's right about this?"

Generous with praise; always on the lookout for the positive; contagiously enthusiastic; finds a way to lighten people's spirits. The glass is always half full.

THINKING TALENTS
Peacemaking

"Where is the common ground?"

Looks for areas of agreement; holds conflicts to a minimum; prefers to keep differences to a minimum and search for consensus; will modify own direction in service of harmony.

THINKING TALENTS
Precision

"How can I order this chaos?"

The world needs to be predictable; imposes structure, sets up routines, timelines, and deadlines; needs to feel in control; dislikes surprises, impatient with errors. Control is a way of maintaining progress and productivity.

THINKING TALENTS
Reliability

"How can I do this right?"

Excuses and rationalizations are not acceptable; has to take responsibility for anything committed to; reputation for conscientiousness and dependability. Easily frustrated by what is perceived as other's irresponsibility.

THINKING TALENTS

Seeking Excellence

"How can this be excellent?"

Excellence and efficiency is the measure—doing the best with the least. Everything—people, processes, products—is judged by how to make it better.

THINKING TALENTS

Storytelling

"How can I bring these ideas to life with a story?"

Needs to explain by painting vivid pictures until others are inspired to act.

THINKING TALENTS

Strategy

"What are alternative scenarios and what is the best route?"

Sorts through clutter; recognizes all the possible options; engages in "if this, then that" thinking.

THINKING TALENTS

Taking Charge

"How can I get others aligned with me?"

Likes to be the boss; restless until sharing opinions. Uses confrontation if necessary and naturally directs others into action.

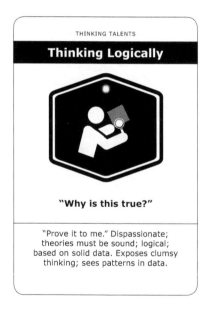

2: ***Now that you have the list of Thinking Talents, let's "Map" them.***
Looking at the following map, circle your child's Thinking Talents. Notice if the Thinking Talents are clustered mostly in one or two quadrants, or spread more evenly among all quadrants.

Analytic ("Why Think")

Making Order
sorting or arranging

Seeking Excellence
tries to make everything great

Fixing It
knowing what's wrong and finding solutions

Thinking Alone
needs time to think something over

Thinking Logically
wanting the facts

Innovative ("Future Think")

Goal-Setting
usually looking for a challenge

Strategy
seeks alternative ways

Innovation
thinking of new ideas, and doing things in new ways

Love of Learning
always needing to learn something new

Storytelling
wanting to write and tell stories

Loving Ideas
searching for ideas that explain things

Procedural ("How Think")

Reliability
dependable, wanting to do things right

Wanting to Win
usually needing to be first

Precision
doing things in an exact and orderly way

Thinking Back
usually looks to the past

Taking Charge
likes to direct or give orders

Get to Action
getting it done

Relational ("People Think")

Connection
likes to connect people, things, or ideas

Feeling for Others
understanding others' emotions and needs

Optimism
thinks positively

Peacemaking
wanting people to get along

Enrolling
making friends easily

Mentoring
helping others learn and grow

Humor making people laugh

Consider:
If your child is strong in Analytic thinking, he or she:
- May first think: What are the facts?
- Loves theories and to analyze problems.
- Thinks being logical is important.
- May overlook feelings or new ways of doing things.

If your child is strong in Procedural thinking, he or she:
- May often wonder: Will I be in control?
- Likes to have things organized and consistent.
- Prefers doing things that have been done before.
- May be uncomfortable trying something new.

If your child is strong in Relational thinking, he or she:
- May often ask: How are others feeling?
- Is concerned mostly with people and relationships.
- Loves to connect and bring people together.
- May overlook facts and planning.

If your child is strong in Innovative thinking, he or she:
- May often wonder: What's a new way to think about this?
- Loves to imagine in the future and come up with new ideas.
- Is eager to try new things.
- May overlook details and practicalities.

It's also useful to notice where your child's blind spots are. Blind spots are quadrants where he or she has no Thinking Talents and often represent where they are most challenged. Consider how you can provide additional support here. For example, as described earlier, Trent was a child with many Thinking Talents in the Procedural quadrant—including "Precision" and "Reliability." His blind spot was in Relational thinking: he had difficulty making friends, and had a hard time sharing his feelings with his mother. Knowing this, his mother, who had many talents in the Relational quadrant, supported him by planning social activities and play dates with other kids.

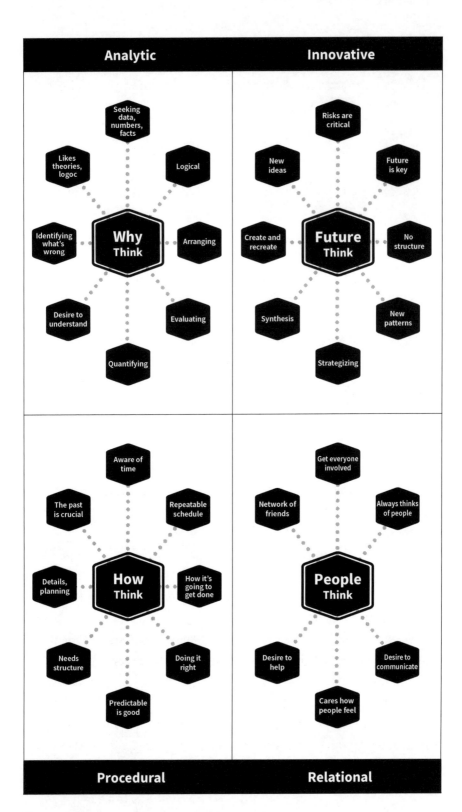

3: *Track and record what you both discover. In the Smart Passport, list your child's Thinking Talents and quadrants.* Make sure to call out any learnings or new revelations based upon what you already know about your child.

4: *Encourage your child to use this map as a framework to solve problems.* Review the tips in Chapter Ten on page 91 on how to best use these talents to overcome challenges and learn something new.

SMART Family Practices
- Post Thinking Talent stickies on the refrigerator, a different color for each family member. Remember, a Thinking Talent is anything a person does that gives him or her energy and has always been easy to do really well. We'd put up a "Strategy" sticky for Jerome, a "Humor" sticky for Lin, a "Storytelling" sticky for Leslie.
- Let each child design a playtime for the rest of the family, based on his or her Thinking Talents. Jerome might have the whole family plan scenarios for the next vacation. Lin might interview each family member about the ways they are smart, then make funny commentary about each. Leslie would tell stories at dinner on Tuesday nights about strengths she noticed in each family member during the week.
- Have each sibling and parent share their S.M.A.R.T. assets and notice how they are different. Teach them that differences are to be respected, not ridiculed.

Final thoughts to keep in mind
Being a parent, and championing your child doesn't end when he or she is eighteen. As children grow, so does the complexity of the challenges they face. This requires the way you express love to grow as well. Joan's son Alex was nineteen and a freshman in college. On Thanksgiving break when he came home, Joan learned that she was being bullied by another student—in person and online. As a mother, she felt fiercely protective and completely powerless. Her attempts to reassure Alex and

remind him that he was loved and brilliant seemed to fall on deaf ears. The more Joan told him about his strengths and talents, the more weak, moody, and teary Alex became. Finally, in desperation, Joan remembered Alex's Smart Passport. She told him to meet her in front of the bathroom mirror. As he stood looking at himself, Joan reminded him that his mind used the KVA pattern. She explained that it was absolutely necessary that he didn't bully himself. The young man slowly placed one hand on the center of his chest and the other on the center of his belly, while looking at his own reflection. Joan placed a headset on Alex's ears so he could listen to a mix of his favorite "Up" songs while looking in the mirror, and then tiptoed out of the bathroom.

Ten minutes later, when he came out, he was no long slumped over or teary. He hugged his mom, kissed her on the forehead and told her he felt better. Joan sat her down on the couch, placing five brightly colored sticky notes on the coffee table. She had written the name of each of his Thinking Talents on each one. She explained that deep inside she knew Alex would figure out a way through this. She suggested that each Talent would have some really helpful ideas about a way Alex could deal with the bullying.

As Joan walked quietly into the kitchen, she touched her own heart. She trusted that rather than reassurance, she had communicated respect to him, respect he would find a way to navigate the challenges in his life.

PART 3:

THINKING PARTNERSHIPS THROUGHOUT THE JOURNEY

"We have no choice now but to think together, to reflect in groups and communities. The question is how to do this, how to come together and hear each other and be touched by the larger intelligence we need."
—Jacob Needleman

CHAPTER NINE:

Drawing Support from Teachers, Coaches, Mentors, and Yourself

> "I not only use all the brains the I have, but all the brains I can borrow."
> — Woodrow Wilson

Teachers, mentors, and coaches carry a heavy load with competing pressures. Many are balancing the increasing push toward standardization and shrinking resources on the one hand, and their real care and concern for children on the other. Some of them intuitively sense that each child learns differently but too often these professionals find themselves without time or support to try new ways of teaching. How can we partner with teachers, coaches and mentors to help our children become all they can be?

The information in your child's Smart Passport and your observations are incredibly valuable for any classroom teacher; their perspective on your child's assets is important as well. Communication between home and schools, however, is all too often reduced to logistical information or coping with crises. In order to bring out the best in children, we must gather and share all that we know about the assets of every child in our mutual care. We need to focus on the right questions: How can each of you help this child learn to trust his or her own mind? How can you all help him or her love learning, and do quality work?

Consider inviting your child to the next parent-teacher conference, so they can be full participants in the learning and difficulties that are being discussed. Beyond these twice-yearly evaluations, find the simplest way to open the lines of communication. If your child has been having trouble in math, and you've made some new discoveries, you might want to write a note to his teacher that says, "I know Luke often gets confused doing multiplication. Here's what's working at home. If we use some kind of objects to lay out the problem so he can work it in his hands, it really helps. He can do about four problems in a row and then it's best if he gets up and walks around." Or you might say to her coach, "We've found that Robin can perform her best if she's given verbal advice with some graphics or diagrams before the swimming race rather than yelling at her during it. Would that work for you?"

Tell your child's teachers, coaches, and mentors what you are working on. Enlist their support in observing your child for more ideas. Share aspects of his or her Smart Passport. One parent told us how helpful it was to find out from a teacher that her child went to lay down on her mat to read. It was something she had never tried at home. Share information from your child's Smart Guide, and continually update it as you get key insights back.

> *"Imagine a world in which every child understands what his or her natural strengths and talents are, how he or she learns and communicates most effectively, how he or she thinks most effectively with others. If you can imagine it, then you can help create a world worthy of your children."*
>
> —Dawna Markova, Ph.D.

Honoring your own role in the journey

A child learns, before he or she walks, to imitate the posture of those adults around him or her. Similarly, if you view life as a constant opportunity to bring out your best, this will inspire your child to want to do the same. The only way to teach respect is to give it—to your children and to those who support your children, including yourself. One of the ways to do this is by respecting your own assets and needs. Stop in the moment when you're feeling most worn down and impatient, take several deep breaths, and bring your mind back to your own S.M.A.R.T. assets:

- **Successes:** Think about a time you've been successful with this child. What were you doing? What was going on? Can you use that now?
- **Mind Patterns:** Is this a situation where you need to say to your child, "You really want some good focused attention right now, but I'm distracted. Can you come back in a half hour and we'll do it then?"
- **Attractions and Interests:** How could what you are doing become more interesting or fun for you? Or do you need a break to do something that would interest you?
- **Resources:** What resources are available to you at the moment? What are you giving to your child that you need to be giving to yourself?
- **Thinking Talents:** What are your Thinking Talents? Which one(s) could be most helpful in this situation?

Here is another idea to try. Stop for one minute and take a "joy break." Return to your senses. Take a deep breath and enjoy this child as you did when he or she was an infant. See, hear, and feel for one minute the miracle of uniqueness that is this child. This one brief moment of enjoying what is will help you with twenty difficult moments of worrying about what is not.

You can also shift your attitude by recalling this parable. Two men were hauling huge stones up a hill. One was swearing and complaining, the other whistling and smiling. The smiling man was asked what made the difference between the two: "Well," he said, "I just remember that I'm building a cathedral." Like the happy worker, when we remember the purpose of our labors with our children, it makes it easier to enjoy them, ourselves and the process itself. As John Breeding writes in *The Wildest Colts Make the Best Horses,* "Always remember that this job of caring for and supporting the development of our young people is profoundly significant, important and valuable."

Enjoying our children is good for them as well as us. "When we feel valued and cared about, our brains release the neurotransmitters of pleasure, endorphins and dopamine. This helps us enjoy our work more," writes Eric Jensen in *Teaching with the Brain in Mind.* Jensen goes on to say that these neurotransmitters also increase the possibility that we will learn well and be less likely to be frustrated.

The asset-focused approach described in this book is just that—an approach, a way of thinking about yourself and your children that can help you maximize their potential. The more you practice, the more you will learn. But because this requires thinking in a way we haven't been trained to, it can be challenging. We adults have been so focused on what's wrong that we too have trouble in seeing what's right. Be gentle with yourself as you go through this journey.

CHAPTER 10:

Taking It Further: Additional Tools and Tips

"It's never a failure to not realize what we dream. The failure is to fall short of dreaming all we might realize."
—Dee Hock

Because it is easier to coach someone else on how to utilize their child's assets to overcome challenges, small groups provide a great structure to help us as we help one another. Here are two group structures to consider forming.

"Think-u-bators"
Think-u-bators can be formed with just a single other person, your whole family, or a small group of friends—groups of four to six seem to be most effective. You can also teach kids eight and older to do it with one another. Here's how it works:

- One individual is the focal person. He or she names the child's assets or reads them from the Smart Passport. (A child can do this for him or herself).

- Then the focal person describes the challenge, limitation or difficult situation the child is struggling with. This should take no more than five minutes. Everyone else just listens in silence. (Be sure you don't try to persuade everyone else that the situation is impossible or they won't be able to think on your behalf!)

- The focal person takes notes using their favorite method—a pen and paper, laptop, iPad, etc. The rest of the group brainstorms as many ideas as possible for how the described assets could be used in this situation. The focal person says nothing, just takes down what everyone else is saying without commenting. The pace must be slow enough that the focal person can capture each idea, but fast enough to keep ideas flowing, and lively. This is not a debate or discussion. The purpose is to generate as many ideas as possible so the focal person can break through the limitations of their own thinking.

- Later the focal person can read the list and decide which suggestions to use. More ideas may also start bubbling up in his or her own mind.
- Switch roles. If doing this in a small group or with your family, each person takes a turn as the focal person.

Smart Groups

The purpose of Smart Groups is to have a regular place to reinforce and support parents utilizing an asset-focused approach no matter where they live. You can create a Smart Group in your community, using the suggested guidelines below:

- There should be a small number of people (no more than eight).

- The group should be of short duration—for example six weeks—with an option to continue if the group wants.

- Ideally the group should meet weekly, for an hour or so, so that the commitment of everyone is possible.

- No money should be charged.

- All members of the group should decide on ground rules so each person feels completely safe. For example: confidentiality; right not to speak if you don't want to; no criticizing.

- The group should decide where it wants to meet, who will be the leader, and if they want to rotate leadership.

- The leader is responsible for making sure the ground rules are followed, keeping time, and staying on task.

- Each member should bring a photo of his or her child or children to place in the center of the circle.

- Meetings should begin with a sharing of members' successes and learnings from the previous week.

- Each week there should be an opportunity for each person to be the focal person in a Think-u-bator, as well as a discussion about how people could support each other. For example, several parents could go to support someone in a parent-teacher meeting. Parents could also broaden each other's knowledge of available resources—podcasts, books, classes.

- At the end of every meeting, there should be a brief period of acknowledgment where each person names what he or she and others specifically did to contribute to its success.

If you create a Smart Group, please send your successes, learnings, and ideas to us via the SmartWired web site so others around the world can learn from your experience.

Supporting your child's Mind Pattern
The following suggestions will help you and your child use his or her Mind Pattern to maximize learning, communication, and self-esteem.

AKV PATTERN: Auditory, Kinesthetic and Visual			
A1	🗣	Focused Thinking	**Auditory** to Trigger Concentration
K2	✋	Sorting Thinking	**Kinesthetic** to Trigger Concentration
V3	👁	Open Thinking	**Visual** to Trigger Concentration

AKV:
- Help monitor their physical energy, so they know when they need to move or play with something in their hands.
- They usually love to be read to so make this a regular practice if possible early on.
- Once they can read independently, they may benefit from tracing words on a page or reading aloud; their comprehension and memory will increase when combined with kinesthetic elements.
- For writing, dictation can be helpful, along with writing stories of their experiences.
- They can best memorize by repeating material verbally.
- When learning a new skill, talk about it with them first then let them do what they've just heard, and allow them to talk about it.
- To help them organize and concentrate, allow them to tell you what they will do rather than writing it down themselves.

AVK PATTERN: Auditory, Visual and Kinesthetic

A1	👄	**Focused Thinking**	**Auditory** to Trigger Concentration
V2	👁	**Sorting Thinking**	**Visual** to Trigger Concentration
K3	✋	**Open Thinking**	**Kinesthetic** to Trigger Concentration

AVK:
- They will want to talk through things and might not get enough airtime at school; set aside time to listen so they feel understood.
- Involve them in discussions about decisions that affect them.
- They organize best by talking about what needs to be done, and jotting down notes.
- They memorize best by saying material repeatedly, and referring to visuals.
- Allow them to make choices in what they participate in physically and in sports, and allow them to learn privately or in small groups.
- Encourage them to plan variety into their schedules; they may get bored doing repetitive tasks for long periods of time.

KAV PATTERN:		Kinesthetic, Auditory and Visual	
K1	✋	**Focused Thinking**	**Kinesthetic** to Trigger Concentration
A2	👂	**Sorting Thinking**	**Auditory** to Trigger Concentration
V3	👁	**Open Thinking**	**Visual** to Trigger Concentration

KAV:

- They will remember most easily when they have a chance to handle something or have an experience. Field trips can be very significant in their learning.
- Making models or playing with clay will reinforce class discussions or textbook chapters.
- Encourage them to play outside or do sports before tackling homework; this will make concentration easier when it's time to sit down and work.
- Allow them to jiggle or move (like in a rocking chair) when reading or doing visual tasks.
- To help them with writing, encourage them to write stories about personal experiences. Initially it may help for you to take dictation.
- Their study space is very important to them; allow them to organize it how they like and make things comfortable.

KVA PATTERN: Kinesthetic, Visual and Auditory

K1		Focused Thinking	**Kinesthetic** to Trigger Concentration
V2		Sorting Thinking	**Visual** to Trigger Concentration
A3		Open Thinking	**Auditory** to Trigger Concentration

KVA:
- Allowing them to be active or do a physical project after school will help them concentrate on homework afterwards.
- They may need quiet time to process a highly verbal school day, and in order to study.
- Field trips and hands on experiences are often their best learning environments.
- Words can be slow to come; when doing presentations, allow them to use notes, props they can hold, or to move around.
- Encourage them to be in motion while reading; a rocking chair or standing up will help.
- Experiment with them to find a way to move their bodies so they can stay engaged while listening for long periods of time (clay or other props can help).
- Help them create a study space where they can both move around, and be comfortable while sitting. They may need quiet, or at least to choose their own music.

VKA PATTERN:		**Visual, Kinesthetic and Auditory**	
V1	👁	**Focused Thinking**	**Visual** to Trigger Concentration
K2	✋	**Sorting Thinking**	**Kinesthetic** to Trigger Concentration
A3	🗣	**Open Thinking**	**Auditory** to Trigger Concentration

VKA:

- Respect their auditory sensitivity, and encourage their visual strengths. Allow some quiet time after school, and listen patiently as they tell you about their experiences.
- As they have good visual memory, flash cards are a good way for them to learn new words.
- Encourage them to make pictures in their minds of the stories they read and hear.
- Allow them to follow along in books with their finger so they can connect physically with what they see.
- Avoid long verbal explanations when helping or teaching them; they respond best to being shown something and then having the space to try it themselves.
- Oral presentations can be daunting; encourage them to prepare written notes or props to help focus what they will say.
- Help them set up a study area without a lot of visual clutter, and just enough color or things to look at without being distracting.

VAK PATTERN: Visual, Auditory and Kinesthetic

V1	👁	**Focused Thinking**	**Visual** to Trigger Concentration
A2	🗣	**Sorting Thinking**	**Auditory** to Trigger Concentration
K3	✋	**Open Thinking**	**Kinesthetic** to Trigger Concentration

VAK:
- It helps them to read and then discuss what they're reading, so consider reading along with them to support maximum comprehension.
- When learning something new they often need to be shown and talked through the new skill before attempting it themselves, and then doing it one small step at a time.
- Help them break down papers or projects into smaller tasks to help with time management.
- Physical skills and new sports may be daunting at first; allow them to learn in private or in smaller groups. Stories and metaphors can help them learn (e.g. "Pretend your body is a clock, put your hands at 10:00 and 2:00…")
- They are very engaged visually so allow them a space to display photos, poems or stories they've written, etc.
- They may have trouble concentrating amongst visual clutter, so help them to set up a neat workspace for homework.

Supporting your child's Thinking Talents

You have a list of your child's Thinking Talents but might wonder how best to use them. Here are suggestions on each Thinking Talent and the best way you can help your child use them to flourish.

CONNECTION: Connecting people or ideas. Combines different ideas or people into something new or larger.

- This child will likely have social issues that s/he will defend strongly. Listen closely to know what these issues are.
- S/he is likely to have a strong faith. Your knowledge and acceptance of his/her spiritual position is important.
- Encourage this child to build bridges to different groups in school or after school programs. S/he should excel at showing different people how each relies on the other.
- S/he likes to feel part of something larger than him/herself.

ENROLLING: Making new friends easily. Enjoys the challenge of meeting new people and getting them excited about something.

- Try to give this child a chance to meet new people every day. Strangers energize him/her.
- Find activities where s/he can be a goodwill ambassador—for a school, a church, an after-school activity.
- Look for chances for this person to sell something s/he believes in.

FEELING FOR OTHERS: Understanding other people's emotions and needs. Instead of thinking of oneself, thinks of others.

- Ask this child to help you know how others in the family or classroom are feeling.
- Before making a decision that affects him/her, ask how s/he feels about it. For him/her, emotions are real and must be weighed when making decisions.

- Do not overreact when s/he cries. Tears are part of his/her life. S/he may sense the joy or tragedy in another person's life more strongly than even that person does.
- Ask him/her: "What is your gut feeling about what we should do?"
- Arrange for him/her to be with positive people. S/he will pick up on these feelings and be motivated.

FIXING IT: Knowing what's wrong and finding solutions. Likes to make things better.

- Ask this child what might go wrong with an idea or a plan.
- Offer your support when s/he meets a problem. S/he may feel terrible if the situation remains unresolved.
- S/he may come across as negative when pointing out what could go wrong. Help him/her learn to communicate insights in a positive way.
- When s/he fixes a problem, make sure to celebrate the achievement.
- Ask him/her in what ways s/he would like to improve. Agree that these improvements should serve as goals for the following six months.

GET TO ACTION: Wants to stop talking or thinking, and "Just do it." Impatient for action, must make something happen.

- This child wants to do, do, do.
- Let him/her know that you know s/he is a person who can make things happen and that you will be asking him/her for help at key times. Your expectations will energize him/her.
- When s/he complains, talk about what s/he can do right away.

GOAL SETTING: Always looking for a challenge. The daily drive to accomplish something and meet a goal.

- When there are times that require extra work, call on this child.
- Recognize that s/he likes to be busy and needs a goal to work toward.
- Whatever s/he is doing, there needs to be a way to measure success.
- When this child finishes a task, s/he will be much more motivated if you give praise for past achievement and then a new goal.
- Ask questions such as "How late did you have to work to get this done?" S/he will appreciate this kind of attention.

 HUMOR: Making people laugh. Enjoys finding what is funny about situations and sharing it.

- Look to this child to lighten a situation. Include him/her in group or team situations where the humor can be a valuable asset.
- Be aware that s/he can't help joking, so don't take it as a challenge to your authority.
- Encourage him/her to use humor in constructive ways—in class presentations, sports, etc.
- Offer opportunities to showcase his/her talent (in class, at the dinner table, during snacks) so s/he will have appropriate outlets.
- Although they may be overshadowed by the constant jokes, don't forget that this child has several additional Thinking Talents—look for ways to utilize those other strengths as well.

INNOVATION: Thinking of new ideas, and doing things in new ways. Loves to create and do things that have never been done before.

- This child tends not to look back. When you want his/her best thinking, say, "Imagine it is a year from now and you have gotten exactly what you wanted. What will have happened? How have you gotten from A to B?"
- When s/he is stuck, ask: "What are all the ways you could you do this?"
- Recognize that it may be challenging for him/her to follow routine ways of doing things because s/he quickly loses interest if it's not new. Challenge him/her to continue to find ways to keep things interesting.

LOVING IDEAS: Searching for concepts that explain things. Fascinated by new ideas, theories, and concepts.

- This child has creative ideas. Be sure to value them.
- Try to feed him/her new ideas, and ask what s/he has been thinking about recently.
- Give him/her books, audiotapes, lectures, performances that will offer new ideas.

LOVE OF LEARNING: Always needing to learn something new. Energized by learning new things.

- Explore new ways for him/her to learn. It is the process of learning, not the result that energizes him/her.
- Help him/her track the learning progress by identifying milestones or levels that s/he has reached. Celebrate these milestones.
- Ask him/her "What have you been learning about X?"
- Ask him/her to lead discussion groups or presentations at school or after school, and to share with the family what s/he has learned.

MAKING ORDER: Sorting or arranging. Enjoys putting many things into the best form. Organizes what's messy.

- Give this child a chance to arrange things—people, flowers, table settings, rooms.
- S/he will thrive in situations where s/he has many things going on at the same time and there is a need to arrange them in the right order.
- When s/he is stuck, ask: what order is it best to do this? How else could this be arranged?
- Find a productive use of this child's ability to sequence things and events.

 MENTORING: Helping others learn and grow. Recognizes possibilities in others and wants to help them succeed.

- Ask this child to tell you about his/her friends: what they are learning, how they are growing.
- Give him/her opportunities to mentor and coach.
- Set him/her up as the one to give recognition to others.
- Be aware that s/he may protect a problem pal long past the time when others would have given up.
- Notice when and how you may need to relieve him/her of the responsibility for other people.

 OPTIMISM: Thinking positively. Looking on the bright side; always on the lookout for the positive, contagiously enthusiastic.

- This child brings energy wherever s/he goes. Help him/her find ways to use that in school, home, and after school activities: as the head of the debate club, working in a nursing home, etc.
- The glass is always half full for this child. Help him/her to see potential pitfalls in a situation and strategize how to respond. S/he is just not aware of them.

- S/he likes to celebrate. When goals have been reached—a big school project for instance—ask him/her for ideas about how to celebrate.

PEACE MAKING: Wanting people to get along. Prefers agreement and harmony, does not like fighting or arguments of any kind.

- Steer this child as far as possible away from conflict.
- If people are disagreeing or fighting, ask this child how to make peace. S/he is good at helping others find areas where they do agree.
- Don't expect him/her to stand up for him/herself. For the sake of harmony s/he may nod his/ her head or go along no matter what.
- S/he wants to feel sure about what s/he is doing. Help him/her find opinions for the actions s/he wants to take.
- Include music or painting in his or her life as a way of exploring how notes and colors can "make peace with each other."

PRECISION: Doing things in an exact and orderly way. Enjoys being accurate.

- If an event or organization is chaotic, ask him/her to take the lead in planning and organizing it.
- Don't expect him/her to last long in a physically cluttered environment unless s/he has a chance to put it in order.
- Always give him/her advance notice and try not to surprise him/her with sudden changes in plans. Surprises are distressing.
- When there are many things that need to get done in a set time period, remember his/her need to prioritize.
- If forced to be in a situation that requires flexibility, encourage him/her to devise a routine.

RELIABILITY: Dependable, wanting to do things right. Thrives on being responsible.

- This child defines him/herself by his/her ability to live up to commitments. It will be intensely frustrating to be around people who don't.
- S/he defines him/herself by the quality of his/her work. S/he will resist when forced to rush so much that quality suffers.
- Be aware that s/he may be uncomfortable trying something new—s/he wants to do it RIGHT. Ask him/her to identify what the worries are and help work through them.
- Periodically ask him/her what new responsibility s/he would like to assume.
- Help him/her not to take on too much.
- S/he can let go of a task and move on to something new only if you can assure him/her that it will be done right by someone else.

SEEKING EXCELLENCE: Trying to make everything great. Driven to do the best with the least.

- Ask how s/he can personally become excellent in a subject or a sport or in an area of self-improvement.
- Discuss how s/he knows when s/he has done an excellent job.
- Children with this talent dislike inefficient designs and processes. Ask him/her how you can make something better—a school bag, a process in a group, a team.
- Invite him/her to help develop procedures for class projects that would make clear the standards for excellence.
- S/he is always trying to do as many things at once to maximize efficiency. Ask him/her to give you the most efficient way to do three chores at once.

STORYTELLING: Wanting to write or tell stories. Needs to explain things by telling a tale to bring an idea to life.

- Understand that this child is not lying—he/she is creatively using facts to fit the story.
- Explore how his/her storytelling abilities can be developed.
- Ask him/her to help some other children make more engaging presentations.

STRATEGY: Strategizing many ways to think about something. Enjoys thinking about all the possible options: "If this happens, then we can do this or that. Or that."

- This child has the ability to sense problems and their solutions. In a group, at school or in an after school program, ask him/her to sort through all of the possibilities and find the best way forward.
- Give ample time to think through a situation before asking for input. S/he needs to play out a couple of options in his/her mind before voicing an opinion.
- Give him/her some financial and/or other constraints and ask him/her to come up with three vacation options, after school activities, chores, or other activities.
- Use role-plays and simulations to allow this child to utilize this talent in school.
- Ask him/her to help you with a real challenge you have. For instance, what is the best strategy for me to decide what car to buy next?

TAKING CHARGE: Likes to direct or give orders. Enjoys taking over and telling others what to do.

- Look for situations where this child can give orders and tell others what to do.
- S/he will not like to be supervised too closely.
- If s/he starts bossing siblings, friends, parents, meet him/her head-on. Confront directly with specific examples.

- Never threaten unless you are 100 percent ready to follow through. You most likely will end up in a power struggle.
- Understand that his/her assertiveness is part of what makes him/her powerful – as long as s/he doesn't get aggressive or offensive.

THINKING ALONE: Needs to think something over by him or herself. Usually reflecting and thinking through things solo.

- Don't expect this child to make snap decisions. Give him/her time to think through all the pros and cons.
- Whenever possible, give notice far in advance that some action or decision will be need to be made.
- Encourage him/her to take alone time when s/he can simply muse.
- Engage this child in discussions about his/her strengths. S/he will enjoy the chance to think about him/herself.

THINKING BACK: Usually looking to the past. Enjoys thinking about history and what has happened.

- When you ask this child to do something, take time to explain the thinking that led to your decision. S/he needs to understand the why of something.
- Turn to him/her to review what has been done and what has been learned up to now.
- When s/he's stuck, ask her to recall when s/he in a similar situation. What did s/he do that could help now?

THINKING LOGICALLY: Wanting the facts. Wants to know the reason and logic. Needs specific data.

- When a decision that affects this child is being made, take time to think through the issues with him/her. S/he will want to know all the facts affecting the choice.
- When speaking to this child, remember to lay out your logic very clearly.

- Recognize and praise his/her reasoning ability.
- This child can see patterns in data. Always give him/her the opportunity to explain the pattern to you.
- Understand that because the accuracy of work is so important to him/her, getting a task done correctly may be more important than meeting a deadline.

WANTING TO WIN: Usually needing to be first. Thrives on competition and comparing self to others.

- Use competitive language with this child. From his/her perspective, life is a contest and the point is to win as much as possible.
- Measure him/her against other people, particularly other competitive people.
- Set up contests for things you want done around the house: "I can beat you to the car," "I bet you can't set the table in two minutes." Then give rewards—stickers, stars, points, for winning.
- Find places where s/he can win. Remember, s/he doesn't compete for the fun of competing, s/he competes to win.

Additional reading and online resources

There are also a number of wonderful books and web sites/blogs that you might enjoy as resources for your parenting journey. A partial list of our favorites is below with a growing list available on the SmartWired website as well:

Supporting your child:

Learning Unlimited by Dawna Markova and Anne Powell
An asset-focused approach to helping kids with homework.

Einstein Never Used Flashcards by Roberta Michnick Golinkoff and Kathy Hirsh-Pasek
Presents a variety of research to show that play is the best way for children to learn as well as helping them develop social and emotional skills, and offers many suggestions to enhance the love of learning in young children.

Parenting from the Inside Out by Daniel J. Siegel, M.D. and Mary Hartzell, M.Ed.
Based on new research in neurobiology and psychology, offers science-minded adults an approach to raising compassionate and resilient children by looking at their own childhood experiences.

The Wildest Colts Make the Best Horses by John Breeding, Ph.D.
Helps you know what to do if school officials label your child a problem.

Right-Brained Children in a Left-Brained World by Jeffrey Freed, MAT and Laurie Parsons.
Concrete help for those who have been labeled ADHD in dealing with teachers and helping the child uncover his or her unique talents.

Teaching with the Brain in Mind by Eric Jensen.
The most up-to-date, practical, easy-to-understand research on learning and the brain.

The Whole-Brain Child by Daniel J Siegel, M.D. and Tina Bryson Ph.D.
12 Revolutionary Strategies to Nurture Your Child's Developing Mind, Survive Everyday Parenting Struggles, and Help Your Family Thrive.

Your Guide to a Happier Family by Adele Faber & Elaine Mazlish
Communication skills that build better relationships between adults and children.

Parenting with Purpose by Lynda Madison, Ph.D.
Providing parents with the principles needed to guide the interaction with their child beginning in the toddler years, thereby laying the foundation for a happy, independent adult.

Easy to Love, Difficult to Discipline by Becky A Bailey, Ph.D.
Focusing on self-control and confidence-building for both parent and child, Dr. Bailey teaches a series of linked skills to help families move from turmoil to tranquility

The Science of Parenting by Margot Sunderland
How today's brain research can help you raise happy, emotionally balanced children.

Elevating Child Care by Janet Lansbury
A guide to respectful parenting starting in the early years.

* Please also visit the Smart Parenting Revolution Facebook page and web site by SmartWired. A collection of daily curated articles and blogs about asset-focused parenting and education.

Supporting yourself:

Collaborative Intelligence by Dawna Markova, Ph.D. and Angie McArthur
An in-depth exploration into working well with others in social and business situations based on intellectual diversity.

I Will Not Die an Unlived Life by Dawna Markova
Inspirational support for reclaiming purpose and passion in our lives.

The Inner Game of Work by W. Timothy Gallwey.
An asset-focused approach to overcoming the inner obstacles that sabotage our efforts to be our best at work.

Trusting Yourself by M.J. Ryan
An asset-focused perspective on the attitudes and behaviors that allow us to trust ourselves more and therefore feel less overwhelmed by life and more able to take action on what matters to us.

To learn more about this approach, to ask specific questions about the children in your life, or to connect with other parents, guardians, coaches and teachers using this approach, go to the SmartWired web site. You and your child, as well as teachers, coaches, and mentors, can all find others there to connect with and use as resources. We are also developing a variety of apps and family tools to support parents and their kids in their learning journey.

About the Creators

As a team of thinking partners, Dawna Markova, Angie McArthur, and Heather McArthur loved working together to create *I Am Smart*. A VAK, KVA, and AVK—grandmother, mother, aunt, and sister—each one brought their own unique perspective, thinking talents, and strengths.

Dr. Dawna Markova, Ph.d.

This is the third book, Dawna (a VAK) has co-authored with Angie. Their other two books, *Collaborative Intelligence: Thinking with People Who Think Differently* and *Relational Intelligence* are being published by Random House in August 2015 and 2016 respectively. An internationally-known author and expert in the fields of learning, perception, and asset-focus, Dawna has written several books, including *A Spot of Grace*, *I Will Not Die an Unlived Life*, *The Smart Parenting Revolution*, *The Open Mind*, *No Enemies Within*, *How Your Child IS Smart*, and *Learning Unlimited*. A passionate advocate for education reform, Dawna has established learning communities around the world—working with leaders, teachers, and parents. As one of the founders of SmartWired, she serves as a thinking partner to CEOs and senior executives around the world. A renowned public speaker, she has been the keynote at several global conferences. Dawna lives in Hawaii with her husband Andy, dogs Hula and Mobi, and cat Ninja.

Angie Mcarthur

Since 1998, Angie (a KVA) has traveled the world to work with children, their parents, teachers, and mentors in creating rich learning environments that bring out a child's best. The author and strategic designer of the SmartWired Activity set and training, her custom interactive programs and workshops have been translated into multiple languages and impacted thousands of children around the world. As a senior partner for SmartWired's affiliate Professional Thinking Partners, Angie has co-facilitated and designed global conferences, keynote speeches, leadership retreats, training programs, and ongoing for organizations from non-profits to Fortune 500s. With the belief that every child has unique gifts, strengths, and potential, Angie is passionate about sharing SmartWired's research and philosophy. She lives with her beloved partner and husband, Dave, and their dog Tele in Park City, Utah.

Editor: Heather McArthur
As the proud mother of Gracie (7) and Elspeth (9), Heather (a AVK) strives to be a true thinking partner with her kids as they navigate school and life. For years she's turned to Dawna and Angie for advice on how to support her family in their learning journey. As the Content Director & Managing Editor for O.C. Tanner—a 2015 Fortune 100 Best Places To Work For company, that helps organizations create great work environments—she tries to balance being a working mom and creating and editing great content. The former managing editor of Conari Press, she lives with her girls and husband, John, in Park City, Utah.

Made in the USA
Middletown, DE
09 September 2016